In a Flash!

*Quick Insights and Strategies
to Become a Better Boss
and a Remarkable Human Being*

by Ann Tardy

In a Flash!

Quick Insights and Strategies to Become a Better Boss and a Remarkable Human Being

by Ann Tardy

ISBN #: 978-0-9795857-4-6

Cover and interior designed by Trish Fullerton Design

Make the most of yourself by fanning the tiny, inner sparks of possibility into flames of achievement.
~ Golda Meir

If you want to improve the organization, you have to improve yourself.
~ Indra Nooyi

Imperfection is beauty, madness is genius, and it's better to be absolutely ridiculous than absolutely boring.
~ Marilyn Monroe

To everyone who is committed to making a difference for others
and the world by becoming a bigger, better, bolder version of yourself.

CONTENTS

. . . .

Welcome to Flash!

Four years ago I decided to write one article each week. Why? To stay connected with my tribe, to attract new members to the tribe, to practice my writing skills, and to say something that makes us think differently while inspiring us to be better today than we were yesterday.

I called it Flash! because of my intention to send out into the world a flash of mentoring, a flash of wisdom, and a flash of inspiration!

I set a 300-word limit. Why? Because we're all inundated with information and demands on our attention. I want to contribute, not distract unnecessarily. This word limit forces me to be organized with my thoughts, efficient with my words, and intentional about my content. It demands that I stick to one topic, one concept, and one pint in each article. Weekly I am reminded of Mark Twain's words: "If I had more time, it would have been shorter."

I committed to write only positive, uplifting articles that inspire, contribute, and provoke thoughts and new actions. Why? Because there is enough negative, polarizing, angry content circulating out there already. I do not need to add to it.

I also decided to use this platform authentically. By sharing my mistakes, my insights, and my wins, I am on this journey with you. I don't have it figured out yet. I'm just the one holding the flashlight at the moment.

My Cousin Lynn said to me recently, "You must pay attention in every situation for something to write about." And she's right! I'm constantly looking to see what might be "flash-able." In every adventure, I'm paying attention to what I'm noticing, experiencing, and discovering. My commitment is to synthesize my learnings and share them with you in hopes that they make a difference.

Ultimately, that's all any of us hope to do: make a difference. Whether we are bosses, parents, peers, partners, friends, or strangers, we just want to matter. Thank you for being on this journey with me. Thank you for your comments, contributions, and connections. And thank you for sharing this commitment we each have to be better today than we were yesterday.

Chapter 1

GOALS & COMMITMENTS

Committed or Contingent

For over 208 weeks, I have officially penned a weekly article called "Flash!"

But I didn't start out with a 208-week commitment. Instead I started by committing to write a new idea or perspective for that week...and possibly the next week (if I had time).

Here's what I discovered:

- We can start with an easy commitment and strengthen it as we go.
- Be proud not perfect – go when we're proud, let go of perfection, and then evolve it.
- By showing up consistently, others start expecting us to show up, and that fortifies our commitment.
- The more committed we are, the less we defer to contingencies (like time and other excuses).
- No one cares about our intentions or our contingencies – they have their own.
- It makes a difference when we actually show up.

When we're committed, we deliver in spite of our circumstances. But when we acquiesce to those circumstances, our commitment wanes and withers.

Choose commitment. Dominate contingencies.

What If Achieving the Goal Doesn't Matter?

What if the power of setting goals lies not in accomplishing them but in who we have to become to accomplish them?

When we earnestly pursue goals, we change our behavior, we improve our processes, we take on new actions.

To be successful in our goals, we have to become the person it takes to be successful.

And ultimately becoming that person is as important as (if not more than) accomplishing the goal.

Think of any goal you have achieved. Who did you become to achieve that goal?

Did you become:

- a morning person
- organized with your time
- determined and perseverant, even brazen
- focused on your health, your skills, or your passion
- confident and direct in your interactions with others
- more courageous

Admittedly, all of these changes and improvements we make in the pursuit of a goal are possible without the goal, but the goal *seduces* us into action.

When I have a goal to write a book or complete a bike ride, I become militant about my time, clear about my priorities, and purposeful in my conversations. I am switched on. I ask better questions. I am more enthusiastic.

Pursuing the goal of writing a book or cycling a part of the country makes me a more efficient, effective, and engaged person.

So while accomplishing the goal is our reward for the grit, perhaps it's not about the goal. Perhaps it's about setting compelling goals that lure us into becoming bigger, better, bolder versions of ourselves.

Motion is the Goal

I have been editing. Not a document, a speech, or a manuscript... my life.

I've been editing my office, my closets and cabinets, my drawers, my car, my clothes, my music, my news consumption, my books, my friends, and even my time.

I don't know if I'm more shocked by the things I'm finding (I still had medicine dated 2009) or by the reality of what I have been tolerating. I have been operating around piles (literal and figurative) for years without taking action.

I didn't start the year with a resolution or a goal or even a vision of editing my life. I started the year with a commitment to Get Stuff Done. To do something instead of nothing. To move.

Can motion actually be the goal?

Research shows that happier people move more. A study of over 10,000 people using wearable and mobile technology revealed that people can increase their mood just with slight physical activity – by moving!

It's not about exercise, running a marathon, or scaling mountains. It's about staying in motion.

And my promise to stay in motion has led to editing my life.

Here are some other simple ways to start moving:
- Take the stairs
- Stand up when the phone rings
- Walk around while talking on the phone (stop looking at emails!)
- Sit strong and stand strong by engaging the abs
- Throw away expired medicine and food
- Fix or discard broken items
- Recycle "someday" clothes ("someday I'll wear this")
- Greet people with a smile and confident handshake
- Wave to people across the street
- Get a dog (ok, not simple, but guaranteed motion)

When our motion impacts our emotion, it's time to start moving... whatever that looks like for you!

Got Current Best Thinking? Move Forward!

I asked Bob why he hadn't launched his program yet. He replied, "I'm still gathering information." I said, "Bob, you're not launching a rocket into space. You're launching mentoring into the company. You need to move with your current best thinking."

Bob had become an Information Curator: collecting and guarding information like works of art in a museum. Bob had spent months socializing his idea, gathering data, organizing focus groups, scheduling committee meetings, benchmarking, planning, and analyzing.

But to launch his program, he needs to become an Information Broker: one who takes action to set information in motion.

Information Brokers are like weathermen. They announce the weather with the current best information they have. If the winds shift, the temperature goes up, or the rain clouds roll in, they update their forecast.

Like a weatherman, we don't need perfect information to move forward.

And, for many of our decisions, taking action is critical in order to improve our current best thinking. So what causes our information curating? Fear of being judged, criticized, blamed...

To mitigate this fear and move forward:
- Call it a pilot, a test, a trial, a phase 1 (everyone forgives a pilot!)
- Ask for feedback to improve it
- Seek advice, perspectives, and ideas from others
- Re-evaluate, course-correct, make adjustments

To be successful, we need to move forward with our current best thinking. And when our current best thinking evolves based on new information, we'll have future best thinking, and then we'll evolve our actions accordingly.

If you run a team or an organization, notice when people are curating information:
- Ask them: What is your current best thinking?
- Encourage them to take action based on that

- Suggest they launch a pilot, a test, a trial
- Implore them to seek ideas to fuel their future best thinking

And then be ready to forgive an incorrect weather forecast.

Skip the Resolutions. Create a Polar Bear Plunge

January has the potential to dishearten even the most optimistic. Holiday decorations come down. Rejected Christmas trees skirt the curbs. The days are short.

And on top of all that, we're supposed to declare some grandiose resolution to fix whatever is wrong with us.

But declarations don't create sustainable change! Only actionable learning does.

Traditionally, we learn by reading books, listening to speakers, observing leaders, but research proves that we implement:

- only 5% of what we read, hear, and see
- but a stunning 90% of what we experience

So the secret to igniting our spirits in January and our learning throughout the year is *immersion*. We need to plunge into experiences, experiments, activities, and adventures.

What we need is a Polar Bear Plunge!

People have been jumping into icy cold water in the winter since 1904 in what is now known as a "Polar Bear Plunge." Why?! Typically to raise money for charitable organizations, and personally, for the adrenaline, the challenge, and the experience.

So instead of focusing on resolutions to fix what doesn't work, let's create our own Polar Bear Plunge.

What new experiences, experiments, activities, or adventures can we create this year for ourselves and our people?

Examples:

- Join Toastmasters
- Volunteer for Habitat for Humanity
- Sign up for lessons (instrument, language, dance, motorcycle)
- Lead an event, a team, or a project
- Serve as a Mentor
- Try a new exercise class

- Register for a race
- Teach a workshop
- Travel
- Informationally interview leaders
- Write an article
- Say yes! to a challenge

For learning that transforms, it's time to take the plunge!

Experiences are the new resolutions.

Why Cousin Lynn Crossed a Finish Line Every Month

In January 2017, my Cousin Lynn created a goal to compete in a race every month for the entire year.

When resolutions were inescapable, this sounded aspirational. But as the months rolled by, her resolve became noteworthy.

More than half of Goal-Chasers fail, quick to blame circumstances or their lack of motivation or willpower. But Goal-Catchers are successful because of their commitment, not because of their circumstances, motivation, or willpower.

Here's how Cousin Lynn stayed committed month after month:

1. **Publicly Declare the Goal.** Announcing it to friends and family creates the social and internal pressure to stick to it. (Psychologists call this the Rule of Commitment.)

2. **Construct Smaller Goals.** A race-a-month conveniently frames smaller goals.

3. **Celebrate Progress and Small Wins.** Every month she sends me her crossing-the-finish-line picture, and I cheer.

4. **Constantly Eliminate Barriers.** The winter offered no races, so she flew to a warmer city to compete.

5. **Be Intentional.** Every month she researches and identifies the race for the next month.

6. **Persevere.** The summer was booked with family obligations, so she trained around them. (When I was in town, she had us visiting on bicycles!)

7. **Be Resilient.** When August's mud-run was cancelled, she quickly signed up for a 5K.

Cousin Lynn didn't just make a New Year's resolution. She made a commitment (a promise to herself!) that had her consistently taking actions instead of making excuses.

Whether the goal is personal or professional, being committed differentiates the Goal-Chasers from the Goal-Catchers.

I Ride to Get Uncomfortable

I just completed a 783-mile bike ride from Crater Lake to Yosemite.

Since 2011, I've cycled from SF to NJ, from Key West to Maine, and from Seattle to San Diego.

Why? Because I love the adventure. I love being outside. I love experiencing the country. I love the challenge. And I love how strong I feel pedaling across the map.

At the core, however, I ride to get uncomfortable.

I've learned that when I'm not paying attention, my life tends to drift toward convenient, habitual, and comfortable.

But my world only expands when I'm uncomfortable.

To get uncomfortable, we have to intentionally create it through our commitments. For me, training every morning, rearranging work, leaving my family, and traversing unknown roads, hills, countless cars, and strangers while sitting on a less-than-cozy bike saddle for hours, day after day, through extreme weather is physically, emotionally, and mentally uncomfortable.

Remarkably, each time I get uncomfortable, my confidence, my courage, and my self-awe soars.

And through each experience, I discover a renewed appreciation for and trust in my team, my family, and myself. That's always worth a few saddle sores!

What do you do to get uncomfortable?

Chapter 2

GROWTH & SELF-DEVELOPMENT

You're Perfect and You Can Improve

Sōtō Zen Buddhist monk Shunryū Suzuki said:

"You are perfect just as you are, and you could use a little improvement."

There's nothing wrong with us!

Yet our world constantly reminds us that we are broken and need fixing:

- Report cards: here's your grade and where you fell short
- Commercials: here's what's wrong with you and how our product will fix it
- Feedback: here's my "constructive criticism" to change you

But if we start with the notion that we are perfect as we are, we could springboard from our strengths, instead of flail from our flaws.

With "perfect as we are" as our anchor, we can enthusiastically seek suggestions, feedback, ideas, and input from others by asking, "How can I improve from here?"

Without a need to defensively protect our ego, we can welcome suggestions and ideas, not as judgments or criticisms, but as contributions and building blocks. Each block helping us to become bigger, better, bolder versions of ourselves – to be even more perfect.

So how do we get a little improvement? By seeking advice, perspectives, and ideas from others through:

- mentoring and being mentored
- coaching and being coached
- attending classes and trainings
- reading voraciously
- joining mastermind groups

Now consider using this mindset to lead others: our people are perfect as they are, and they could use a little improvement. From here our job is to add the building blocks that contribute to our people becoming bigger, better, bolder versions of themselves. That's the secret to becoming the boss people want to work for!

Just by starting with perfect and improving from there.

Do You Know Your Blind Spots?

While operating a vehicle, a blind spot is hazardous. Caused by weather conditions or car design, it's the area while driving that we just cannot see without intentionally adjusting our view.

Similarly, blind spots while leading are also hazardous. Caused by our oblivion or unawareness, they are the aspects of our personality that we do not or cannot see. For example, we may regularly denigrate people on our team, without even realizing it.

In *To Kill a Mockingbird*, Atticus tells Scout that Mr. Cunningham is basically a good person with blind spots, because he couldn't see his own racism toward Tom Robinson.

How can we discover our human blind spots? Adjust the mirror and shift the view:

- engage a Mentor
- use a 360 assessment
- re-examine recent performance reviews
- inspect the results we are producing personally and professionally
- explore our interactions with others at work and in life

Other people typically see those facets of our personality that we unconsciously don't see or intentionally don't want to see – our idiosyncrasies, habits, behaviors, and actions.

Our ignorance is not bliss; it's dangerous. Just because we can't see our blind spots does not mean they don't exist. Whether we are driving or leading, remaining unaware of our blind spots puts us at risk of damaging cars and relationships, respectively.

So what can we do about our blind spots? Drive and lead with more intentionality, cognizance, and compassion.

We don't know what we don't know is simply lazy; we don't know what we don't examine.

Are You Comparing Your Insides to Other People's Outsides?

Marcia Washington, an Australian musician and songwriter, received Best Female Artist and Breakthrough Artist awards in 2010. She is so popular in Australia that she is known monoymously as "Washington." She sings and plays piano and guitar. She's young, adorable, stylish, and living her passion. She is the envy of many.

What we don't see on the outside, however, is Marcia's insecurity over her speech challenges. When she's not in front of an audience, Marcia stutters.

Alcoholics Anonymous members often quote the axiom: "Don't compare your insides to other people's outsides."

Our feelings (our insides). Their appearances (their outsides).

When we compare our self-doubt (our insides) to other people's bravado, possessions, adventures, and Facebook updates (their outsides), we sabotage our confidence and risk our success.

The reality is that Facebook posts do not reveal the whole story. People paint a positive self-portrait in order to salvage their self-esteem.

So how do we stop the seemingly inevitable comparison?

- Break the voyeuristic addiction to social media
- Up the compassion quotient (remember, everyone struggles with something)
- Engage a reality check (reality: every braggart is battling an insecurity)
- Create authentic conversations
- Watch the movie *Inside Out*
- Read the book *Everybody Lies*
- Forgive... ourselves and others

The only person we should be comparing ourselves to is the person we were yesterday.

Are we wiser and kinder today than we were yesterday?

Raise Your Value with Your Voice

Admittedly Warren Buffett was petrified of public speaking. After taking a Dale Carnegie course in 1952, he taught an investment class at a local college to overcome his fears and sharpen this important skill.

Today the Oracle of Omaha asserts, "Effective public speaking instantly raises a person's value by 50%."

Every day we are on various stages speaking publicly:

- Leading a meeting
- Contributing to a conversation
- Delivering a webinar or a workshop
- Reporting results to the boss
- Participating in a conference call
- Mentoring, teaching, coaching

Here are 7 tips to be more effective on any of these stages:

1. **Process in Your Head:** Pause, breathe, sort through your thoughts before opening your mouth. Determine what information most contributes to your current audience.

2. **Get to the Verb:** Don't lead with the backstory. Lead with the action. Then, if your audience is engaged, add some adjectives.

3. **Start with Bullets:** Whether speaking or emailing, you need to demonstrate that you can synthesize information into the important points. The conversation doesn't end with bullets; it's just a compelling place to start.

4. **Involve your Audience:** People support conversations they help create Use questions to involve people in creating the conversation, ex: "Which bullet would you like to know more about?

5. **Use Metaphors and Stories:** People process in pictures, so draw pictures with your words using metaphors and stories for quick comprehension and ultimate retention. (ex: "Speaking in bullets" is a metaphor.)

6. **Listen to their Listening:** Pay attention to the audience's engagement.. are they involved? Are they distracted or confused? Do you need to speed up, slow down, or ask a question?

7. **Practice Constantly:** Every stage, from the phone to the podium, is an opportunity to practice.

When we improve our public speaking, our confidence magnifies, our audiences' confidence in us elevates, and our value inevitably and instantly expands.

Need to Focus? Start Gesticulating and Talking to Yourself Out Loud

I wish I liked to meditate. Supposedly if I had more patience, meditation could help me become more present and focused.

Instead, I distractedly engage in mind-skipping – jumping from thought to thought as I auto-pilot through routine tasks.

Considering our attention spans now clock in at 8 seconds (shorter than goldfish!), it's no surprise that mindfulness has become the new differentiating success skill. It:

- awakens our vigilance
- prevents errors and mistakes
- strengthens trust in relationships

According to Professor Kabat-Zinn at the University of Massachusetts Medical School, mindfulness is simply moment-to-moment awareness.

But we don't need to meditate cross-legged on a pillow to become mindful.

The Japanese have been cultivating mindfulness for centuries with a practice they call "shisa kanko" which literally means checking and calling. As demonstrated by this ritual, the Japanese have an elevated appreciation for the moment.

How does it work? Commonly used in the transportation industry for operational safety, the practitioner points to an important indicator and calls out its status. As an example, a pilot will point to a gauge in the cockpit and call out its position.

Why is it effective? This practice requires a flow of information exchanged among the brain, eyes, hands, mouth, and ears, which demands our heightened attention on a singular focus. In shisa kanko, there is no room for mind-skipping.

The results? A study by Japan's Railway Technical Research Institute reported that using shisa kanko reduces the number of mistakes by 85%!

And as for me, since I started pointing to my car keys and calling out their location before walking into the next room, I have yet to misplace them, saving me untold frustration and wasted time.

When we value the moment, the moment becomes more valuable.

Chapter 3

ACCOUNTABILITY

Answer to Your Commitments Not Your Feelings

When we answer to our feelings, our commitments get short-changed.

Here's what it sounds like:

- I'm too tired to wake up early.
- I'm too busy to work out.
- I'm too mad about that meeting with my boss to be nice to people.
- I'm too overwhelmed to stop and talk to my team members.
- I'm too stressed about my project to support my team's success in their projects.

When we are tired, busy, upset, stressed, irritated, or frustrated, we easily allow those feelings to dictate our actions (or lack thereof). And our excuses spew, spout, and surge.

- Addictions are commitments trumped by feelings.
- Road rage is commitments trumped by feelings.
- Bullying and discrimination are commitments trumped by feelings.

When we answer to our commitments, however, we don't need excuses. We forge ahead in spite of those feelings.

We check our emotions at the door before engaging with our team. We leave our bad moods and frustrations on our desk not with our employees. We refuse to allow those feelings to sabotage our own success.

I have cycled 4,200 miles from SF to NY, 2,600 miles from Key West to Main, and 1,800 miles from Seattle to San Diego. Those commitments had me wake up at 5:00AM to walk my dog and ride a bike before work. Even in the dark, even when I was bone-tired, even in 20-degree weather. Without dauntless goals, I find myself easily making excuses for not cycling: I'm too tired. I have too much to do. I am too cold.

When I look back, it's only because I answered to my commitments and not my feelings that I have pedaled from coast to coast to coast to coast.

You will be an incredible leader when you stop answering to your feelings and start answering to your commitments.

"I Tried" is the New Hall Pass

"I tried" is the purgatory of the corporate world: I didn't succeed, but I didn't fail.

We've come to accept it like a hall pass in grade school.

- I tried to close the sale, but the customer never called me back.
- I tried to finish the report, but I didn't get the information I needed.
- I tried to schedule your performance review, but I got so busy.

The irony is what it really says about us: I tried, but I didn't try hard enough.

We need to ban "I tried" from our vernacular and replace it with "not yet". The word "yet" communicates optimism, persistence, perseverance, and determination. And when we declare "not yet", we maintain ownership for success.

- I have not yet closed the sale.
- I have not yet finished the report.
- I have not yet scheduled your performance review.

So what do we do when others on our team say, "I tried"? We borrow a line from my favorite book on accountability, *The Oz Principles*, and ask, "What do you need to do to get the results you want?"

Let's stop tolerating "I tried" and start raising the bar with "Not yet."

Shifting Consent to Cement

Consent is like mud. It's unstable and easily affected by circumstances, like the weather. But cement is steadfast and impervious.

When people consent, they may agree with an "OK," they might even smile and nod, but they do not own that commitment, because they did not create it.

When people are involved in creating a commitment, they own it. And therefore they are more likely to act consistent with that promise by following through and executing in spite of circumstances.

People cement the commitments they help to create.

And we can actually facilitate their shift in commitment:

1. Instead of summarizing everyone's action items, have people verbalize . . . their promised deliverables to the group.
2. Instead of sending people a list of responsibilities, have them document their own responsibilities on a project and distribute to the group.
3. Instead of dictating commitments, have people declare their own commitments in writing and in meetings.

Through active and public declarations, people shift their commitments from wavering consent to anchored cement. And this invariably increases their success in following through and executing, which inevitably fuels their self-respect, self-esteem, and self-confidence.

Less mud, more cement!

I Have a Love-Hate Relationship With Accountability

I have a love-hate relationship with accountability.

I love the concept. Imagine if everyone operated from a foundation of accountability!

I hate the word. It strikes me like a square on a Business Buzzword Bingo card. Imperative and yet simultaneously righteous:

- *Hold your team accountable!*
- *Who's accountable for this?*
- *Accountability is a core leadership competency.*
- *I exhibit personal accountability.*

Even the definition is haughty: "being answerable or liable for one's conduct."

And it's invariably and erroneously interchanged with the word "responsibility."

The problem is not the audacity of the word or its confusing usage. The problem is that accountability is easy to hide behind. Because people grapple with its meaning, they throw it around without an appreciation for its significance and without ownership for its consequences.

So how can we reignite a commitment to accountability? Bring it back to its essence: accountability is about promises.

- When you are accountable for something, you promise to deliver.
- When I hold you accountable, I am reminding you of the promise you made.
- When you fail to be personally accountable, you broke your promise.
- When you hold a title, you promise to execute the expectations of that title.

A cornerstone of our success is an unrelenting ownership of the promises we make.

That's an accountability I can love again!

Do Less. Obsess More.

Shin Lin, the magician who won *America's Got Talent* this year, so perfected his craft that he made me believe in magic. It was extreme dedication on display... an obsession with extraordinary results.

When UC Berkeley professor Morton Hansen extensively researched the behaviors of top performers, he discovered that they:

- have fewer goals, and
- obsess like crazy over them

In other words, less volume, more intensity. How?

1. Get super clear about what's important.
Have a conversation with your boss, an exploration with a mentor, some reflection on what is essential to your job, your career goals, and your life.

2. Edit the unnecessary.
What distractions, tasks, errands, projects, or clutter can be delegated, decreased, or eliminated? (ex: watching TV, manually paying bills, constantly checking social media)

3. Intensify the efforts.
Obsess over creating extraordinary results in spite of circumstances.

Professional athletes are obsessed with their sport.
Rock stars are obsessed with their music.
Activists are obsessed with their cause.

When I look at my most high-performing times and my most game-changing accomplishments, they've come on the heels of an obsession.

- When I'm obsessed about writing a book, I rearrange my life to write daily.
- When I'm obsessed about a cycling adventure, I pedal every morning... even when it's cold and dark.

But when I'm unclear about what's important, I'm not obsessed with creating extraordinary results. Instead, I'm scattered, rapt with excuses: I'm busy. I'm tired. I'm disorganized. The weather. The traffic. Computer issues...blah blah blah... On *Shark Tank*, Mark Cuban refused to invest in an entrepreneur who appeared resigned to her circumstances. He said, "I can't see writing a check for somebody who finds the excuse rather than finds the opportunity. I'm out."

The question is... would Mark Cuban invest in you today?

Chapter 4

MOTIVATION

Get a Ticket in Your Hand (the Secret to Self-Motivation)

Motivation stems from within. No one else can motivate us.

So what's the secret to motivating ourselves?

Always have a ticket in hand.

My mom has been advocating this approach my whole life. When one adventure ends, she'd say, have a "ticket" in your hand for the next one – a ticket to a show, a vacation, a party, the theater, even a visit with a friend.

To motivate ourselves, we need something to look forward to.

That same advice applies to work. Feeling blah on Monday morning? Bored with that project? Plodding along from one meeting to the next?

Get a "ticket" in your hand by looking forward to something:

- tackling a new project
- working with a Mentor
- contributing to a Mentee
- solving an old problem from a different angle
- bonding with the team
- exploring a new idea
- meeting a new client
- helping an old client with a new solution

Our motivation is up to us – we can activate it or we can let it atrophy. Either way, Monday morning will show up again.

Filtering Naysayers from 50,000 Thoughts

It's been estimated that 50,000 thoughts run through our mind every day. To be successful in any endeavor, those thoughts better support not sabotage us.

Sabotaging thoughts hijack our perseverance. It's our internal naysayer making a case for why we won't be successful.

Instead of conceding, we must gather evidence to counter the naysayer's campaign.

Two strategies:

1. Ferociously focus on your inventory of past accomplishments.

2. Impress yourself. Every day add to that inventory with mini-triumphs:
   - Get up early to exercise before work
   - Mentor someone who needs support
   - Compliment a total stranger
   - Write a heartfelt thank-you note
   - Draft a rock solid proposal

When I use this strategy, I walk around all day mentally applauding myself, not capitulating to some internal critic. And I don't need to boast about my mini-triumphs to anyone else; I just need to trump my internal naysayer.

When I'm so busy woo-hoo'ing myself, I completely ignore my internal naysayer, giving me the energy and endurance to pursue the big, juicy goals.

While most people work hard to impress others, our success is actually served by working hard to impress ourselves. Internal naysayers crumble under the pressure.

Forget WIIFM. Focus on WSIC

Everyone wants to know...what's in it for me (WIIFM)?

Forget it! WIIFM is ephemeral. When the "what" is gone, so is the drive to act.

Shift your focus to why should I care (WSIC) and you'll transform your impact and your results. WSIC is like the north star - it never disappears. It's your passion; it's your purpose; it's the reason you show up.

Some examples of "why should I care" include:

- because my team needs a courageous leader
- because my leaders are starved for new ideas
- because my clients need better solutions to their problems

When you help others shift their conversation from WIIFM to WSIC, you will trigger their need to make a difference. This results in self-motivation - far more powerful and resilient in its impact than any gift card, bonus, pizza party, or company chotchke.

When people know the purpose, feel the importance of that purpose, and recognize how they can make a difference in fulfilling that purpose, then they care. And when people care, they become unstoppable.

At the core of every remarkable result, is a remarkable person, team, or leader who shifted their focus from WIIFM to WSIC.

Experiment With Yes! (like Chico's CEO)

A foundational rule in improvisational comedy is to "start with Yes!" Performers are taught to accept whatever is offered in the dialogue and then expand on it. For example, "I am the king of the world!" "Yes, I can see by the kangaroo on your head that it's going well!" If instead I respond, "No you're not," our exchange quickly deflates.

In life starting with "Yes!" creates positive connection, fuels trust, and inspires creativity and collaboration.

As managers, we instinctively aim for a solution, deferring to our intelligence, experience, tenure, or title. In doing so, we often thwart people's suggestions with our wisdom: "No, that doesn't work." "No, it's not done that way." "No, it's not possible."

But we don't intend to besmirch others' ideas. We actually go-to-no because we naturally feel it's our job to save people, projects, and situations from calamity.

So what would happen if we experimented with Yes!...

Shelley Broader, CEO of Chico's, a women's clothing boutique, did just this. Many retailers abhor Amazon; but Broader realized that condemning the behemoth won't abate its impact. Broader shifted Chico's approach by starting with "Yes!" Instead of resisting the reality of Amazon, she embraced it.

Chico's is now selling its merchandise on Amazon and allowing customers to easily return their purchases in any store or bring them in to be matched with additional items, like accessories.

The result? In-store sales have increased! By starting with "Yes!", Chico's is expanding brand awareness, making it easy to do business with Chico's, and attracting new foot traffic. We too can shift from go-to-no to start-with-Yes! Experiment with these phrases:

- Interesting, tell me more.
- How could we make that work?
- What can we do differently?
- Let's explore that.

The benefit of saying "Yes!" more often? Optimism: a characteristic we crave in leaders.

Chapter 5

BEING REMARKABLE

The Secret to JobLove? Be Remarkable

When I set off on my first cross-country bike ride, I was on a mission to find people who love their job. Convinced they must be remarkable people, I wanted to track down these unicorns and interview them for a documentary I was producing.

But in my quest, I discovered that people aren't remarkable because they love their job. They love their job because they are remarkable!

Being remarkable is the gateway – the secret – to love our work, whatever work we do.

So what does it mean to be remarkable?

- Showing up with a purpose – a battle cry!
- Embracing the uncomfortable
- Contributing to the success of others
- Practicing resilience instead of resistance
- Being courageous
- Standing up when no one else does
- Clapping and cheering for ourselves and others
- Making a difference – in conversations, in moments, and with others

In a recent commencement speech, Bill Gates said, "Believing that the world's serious problems can be solved is the core of my worldview. It sustains me in tough times and is the reason I love my work."

When we are remarkable, the job is merely a conduit that allows us to make a difference. Arguably, the job is not as important as who we are in that job.

When we focus on "is this the biggest difference I can make here?" suddenly the onslaught of policies, procedures, protocols, and processes becomes irrelevant.

People aren't remarkable because they love their job. They are remarkable because they are committed to making a difference with their work. Ultimately, that fuels their joblove.

When Are We Too Old to Be Remarkable?

After delivering my "Rousing the Remarkable" keynote recently, a gaggle of fans swarmed the stage, eager to share with me their remarkable stories.

One woman in particular gave me pause. After thanking me profusely for the inspiring and aspiring message and for a copy of my book, she added, "This is just what my daughter in college needs!"

I promptly asked, "But what about you?"

Without hesitation she replied flatly, "I'm too old to be remarkable," and then left.

A stark reminder that we sometimes fall into ruts, believing it's too late. The only hope for remarkable now resting with our children...

But the reality is there is no expiration date on being remarkable! We are never too old to be courageous, to change, to be uncomfortable, to stand up for others, to make a difference, and to try new things. at work and in life.

These people didn't think they were too old to be remarkable:

- Colonel Sanders launched Kentucky Fried Chicken (after a dozen failed careers) at 65
- Julia Child wrote her first cookbook at 39 and made her television debut at 51
- Vera Wang designed her first wedding dress at 40
- Laura Ingalls Wilder wrote *Little House on the Prairie* at 65
- Samuel L. Jackson landed his role in *Pulp Fiction* (while recovering from drug addiction) at 46
- Grandma Moses started painting at 76
- Cliff Young won his first ultramarathon at 61
- Sam Walton opened the first Wal-Mart at 44
- Ronald Reagan changed careers from actor to politician at 56
- My mom got remarried (with a bachelorette party!) at 70
- My grandpa graduated college at 65 and cycled his first century at 70

Being remarkable is not dependent on age; it's dependent on taking a chance in spite of our age and circumstances.

IN A FLASH!

Would You Cycle Vermont with Prosthetic Legs?

Last weekend I cycled through the glorious hills of Killington, Vermont to raise money for Vermont Adaptive Ski & Sports, a non-profit dedicated to empowering individuals with disabilities to participate in adaptive sports programs and activities. (www.vermontadaptive.org)

Admittedly, it was not an easy ride. The hills were steep and plentiful. The cracks in the road made NJ potholes seem innocuous. It was raining. The wind was in my face. I was freezing. And my legs were feeling sore already.

And then I met the people we were cycling for.... those who could not see, hear, talk, or pedal on their own. They were not, however, on the side of the road. They were on bikes participating in the ride!

- Some volunteer cyclists steered tandem bikes allowing blind cyclists to pedal in the back.
- Other volunteer cyclists used adaptive tandem bikes with cable-actuated rear steering to allow kids with cerebral palsy to participate as passengers at the helm.
- And cyclists with prosthetic legs persevered over the hills using handcycles – recumbent, hand-powered bicycles.

And suddenly I got a jolt of perspective. Some people looked outside on the morning of the ride and decided not to go because it was raining. They didn't want to get wet. They didn't show up because of their circumstances.

I got the privilege of cycling with people who showed up in spite of their circumstances.

And I met the amazing volunteers who showed up without any thought to their own circumstances. They came to create an experience for and boost the confidence of those with disabilities.

Ironically, I registered for the ride to make a difference with some fundraising. But witnessing people's unshakable commitment and courage made the perspective-altering difference for me.

When was the last time you showed up in spite of circumstances?

Rethinking Rock, Paper, Scissors

Leave it to 6-year-olds to reinvent a game that's been around since the Chinese Han Dynasty (206 BC - 220 AD): Rock Paper Scissors.

I was at my nephew's soccer practice when the coach initiated a game of Rock Paper Scissors to see who was going to be up next to practice kicking the goalie.

Suddenly, the boys were shouting, "Dynamite beats rock!" "Sword beats dynamite!" "Handgun beats sword" and "Lava beats handgun!"

Dynamite? Sword? Handgun? Lava? This isn't the game I grew up playing! What happened to the rock, the paper, and the scissors?

I asked the boys, who quickly informed me that the game had been updated. They delighted in teaching me the new rules.

I was being mentored by 6-year-olds.

And more than just introduce me to a new game, they reminded me:

- to be more innovative with simple, everyday tasks and routines
- to be open to the adventure of change
- to experiment with fresh ideas
- to play outside the 3-weapon box
- to pay attention to the new kids on the block

It never occurred to us that we could change the game... but it occurred to them.

It struck me: what other fresh perspectives, new approaches, and original directions am I missing out on?

The older we get, the more wisdom we gather, and the more entrenched we become in using that wisdom.

With fresh perspectives come fresh solutions to old, entrenched problems. We just need to extend the invitation and give people permission to think differently. Pay attention to young people and young employees – they never need permission to think differently. They have the power to expand our world with their perspectives and ideas.

Be Unforgettable

"If you can't be brilliant, at least be memorable," said David Ogilvy, founder of advertising agency Ogilvy & Mather. He wore kilts to work.

According to Media Dynamics, we are bombarded with over 360 messages every day from TV, radio, Internet, newspapers and magazines. We might notice half. We barely recall even less.

In all of this swirling chaos... how will you stand out and be memorable?

In a world that errs on the side of playing it safe, operating inside-the-box, and blending in, being remarkable should be easy. But it's not. The number of naysayers sitting in judgment makes talking on an elevator uncomfortable and appearing on *American Idol* unthinkable.

The secret to being remarkable and unforgettable? Care more about your goals than you do about what other people think of you.

How can we be memorable, remarkable, and unforgettable? By doing the things that others hesitate, neglect, or resist doing. Here are some ways to get started:

- Remember people's names (or re-introduce yourself with a warm smile like my friend Jeannine Kay)
- Send handwritten thank you notes (or even birthday cards, instead of an easy text)
- Pick up the phone to reconnect or express appreciation (instead of a safe email)
- Say "yes!" when I ask you to be a guest speaker (even if you're petrified)
- Put your picture on your resume (even though career counselors tell you not to)
- Channel Mae West when you enter a room of strangers. She would look around and ask, "Who here needs to know me?"
- Make outrageous guarantees, like "You'll love it or it's free." or "I'll work for free for a month so you know we're a great fit!"
- Improve something every day by 1% without being asked
- Give people a "woo-hoo!" shout-out to acknowledge an accomplishment or an effort

- Go out of your way to genuinely compliment one person a day (even if you don't know them)
- When a leader or a speaker asks for a volunteer, raise your hand first; if you really want it, jump up; and if you're really committed, run to the front of the room as fast as you can
- Be kind when others aren't

Being uncomfortable is where remarkable happens. When you can push through the fear – even in small ways – people won't forget you, because secretly they crave the confidence it takes to be as authentic and remarkable as you!

Chapter 6

MAKING A DIFFERENCE

Is This The Biggest Difference I Can Make?

What if we ponder for a moment before walking into a conversation, a meeting, or an altercation, to ask ourselves:

"What is the biggest difference I can make here?"

This specific adage interrupted my reaction to an offensive driver recently. It altered my attitude before schooling a barista on her job. It invariably shifts how I contribute to my team. And, when I employ it early, inspires me to purposefully create my day before it starts.

Is this the biggest difference I can make...

- with this person?
- in this conversation?
- with my time?
- with my thoughts?
- in this meeting?
- with my team?
- in my job?
- with my career?

If we answer "No" to the question, aren't we just wasting our time and energy, shortchanging people of our best selves? Should we really be in that conversation, that meeting, or that job if we're not going to make our biggest difference?

Of course, this notion challenges the hours we squander watching mindless television, surfing social media, reacting with emotional outbursts, or succumbing to other people's drama.

With this question, a reality sets in... how are we choosing to show up, engage, contribute, influence, respond, serve, and lead?

Thus restoring our power to be victor not victim.

A mere burst of self-reflection not only makes us better leaders, it makes us better people.

This Teenager Turned a Transaction into a Transformation

I was in The Art of Shaving store in Charleston S.C. recently purchasing a gift when a teenager entered the store.

His face was clean shaven; his skin smooth, shiny and unblemished, even glowing; and he was beaming. Followed by an entourage of his friends, the teenager made a beeline for John, the store manager.

In front of his friends and a crowd of customers, the teenager gave John a confident handshake and gushed, "Thank you so much. You changed my life."

A little surprised, John proclaimed, "I'm so glad it worked! Thank you for coming back to show me how great your face looks!"

With that, the gaggle of smiling, somewhat embarrassed teenagers and their beaming, clean shaven leader turned and shuffled out of the store.

With pride, John explained, "He was in here a couple months ago with razor burns, in-grown hair, and acne. I spent an hour teaching him how to shave, fitting him with the right razor, and finding a product that would help his skin."

Reflecting on this rare moment, John admitted, "That just made my night."

Everyone in the store felt fortunate to have witnessed this exchange. The teenager went out of his way to appreciate John, who had gone out of his way to mentor the teenager.

John could have just sold the teenager a razor and some lotion. And the teenager could have taken John's advice and never returned.

Instead they each turned a simple transaction into a transformation. How?

- Empathy and compassion
- Shared advice and guidance
- Acknowledgement and appreciation
- Purposeful connection
- Trust

Whether it's a purchase, a conversation, or a meeting, we always have the opportunity to shift a transaction into a transformation... simply by asking, "Is this the biggest difference I can make with this person in this moment?"

It's Just a Bullet on a Resume

Our resumes are dotted with bullets. These bullets highlight our jobs, our roles, our responsibilities, and our results.

But we don't get bullets for dealing with drama, agonizing through murky meetings, navigating difficult bosses, and enduring politics.

We get no extra bullets for suffering. Imagine if we did:

Survived bad boss, backstabbing peers, and inefficient corporate policies

Mistakes, miscommunications, and martyrdom happen *between* the bullets. They only matter when we make them matter.

Every day we get to choose how we function between the bullets: with contention or with intention.

With contention, we are ensnared by crisis, personally offended by others' actions, victimized by their missteps. We operate as if we don't share a common goal.

With intention, we are enchanted by possibility and potential, intoxicated by the difference we can make with and for others, regardless of our title. We are cognizant that our interactions are meaningful and collaborative.

Our job is just a bullet on a resume. What we do in between the bullets is actually all that matters.

Houston Heroes Practice the Ben Franklin Habit

Benjamin Franklin started every day asking himself, "What good shall I do today?"

And during Hurricane Harvey, we watched the Heroes of Houston put Franklin's practice into action:

1. The Bakers Baked All Night
When bakers at El Bolillo Bakery were trapped inside the bakery during the storm, they worked around the clock baking through 4,000 pounds of flour. When the rain stopped, the owner drove the loaves of bread around Houston, donating them to first responders and shelters.

2. Mattress Mack Offered his Inventory
Jim McIngvale (nicknamed "Mattress Mack"), owner of Gallery Furniture chain, opened some of his stores for displaced people to spend the night on his inventory.

3. The Human Chain that Saved a Man
More than 20 strangers formed a human chain to rescue an elderly man from his sinking SUV.

4. A Man in his Boat Rescued Neighbors
When a boat owner set out in his boat to help people, he declared, "I'm going to go try to save some lives." And many boat owners followed in his wake.

5. Houston SPCA Rescued 200 Dogs
Volunteers worked tirelessly to rescue dogs stranded on rooftops and get them into shelters.

6. The Louisiana Cajun Navy Showed Up
Volunteers from Baton Rouge, LA drove their boats 9 hours to help rescue residents.

Why? As one volunteer put it, "The best way you can thank somebody for helping you is to go help somebody else."

Why do we need a Ben Franklin habit? Because it's hard to live a joy-filled life without doing good. It's like letting toxins in the house and then consciously living in the house.

So how do we do good without waiting for a catastrophic event?

- Be interested in others
- Assume good intent
- Let people/cars jump in front of us in line
- Pick up trash regardless of the owner
- Give compliments to strangers
- Send thank you cards
- Offer a helping hand
- Tip generously and often
- Donate regularly

Doing good takes action and intentionality, not just a crisis.

Break the Script

When my stepson Jack was in kindergarten, he decided to be Superman for Halloween. And he wanted his dad to be Batman. So his dad purchased a costume. As he was leaving the house to attend Jack's Halloween parade at school,

I asked, "Where's your costume?"
He held up a bag. "It's in the bag."
"When are you going to put it on?"
He replied, "When I get to the school."
"Where?"
Silence.
"Put the costume on before you leave."
He was aghast, "You want me to drive to the school wearing a Batman costume??"
"Yes. That's what Batman would do.

Begrudgingly he changed into the costume, drove to Jack's school, ignored the gawking parents in the parking lot, and found Jack's classroom. From the other side of the room, Jack saw his dad and shrieked, "My dad is Batman!!" His dad broke the "typical parent" script.

In 1959 social psychologist Erving Goffman argued that we are like actors on a stage, creating and developing scripts that others use to understand us. Scripts are the predictable way that people expect us to behave. When we break the script, we defy people's expectations of us or a situation.

Chip and Dan Heath, authors of *The Power of Moments*, named this "strategic surprise." By showing up in a Batman costume, Jack's dad defied expectations with strategic surprise. As a result, he cemented a memorable experience with his son.

How can we break the script (without a Batman costume)?

- Be calm in a crisis
- Pitch in to help without being asked
- Email our boss praising someone else
- Bring a puzzle to a team meeting
- Send a homemade gift
- Buy coffee for a crossing guard or stranger in line

Where can you break the script to surprise, delight, and cement a memorable experience?

Chapter 7

THE BATTLE CRY

The Battle Cry

"They can take our land but they'll never take our freedom!"

Shouted William Wallace, the villager-turned-folk-hero in Scotland's fight for freedom from Britain, as portrayed by Mel Gibson in the movie *Braveheart*.

That's a Battle Cry! The heroic exclamation we shout as we run onto a battlefield.

Every day we show up at the office to run onto a proverbial battlefield to fight in a proverbial battle.

To ensure nothing short of victory, we need an exclamation to charge into battle together – a purpose.

No mission statement will do that. A mission statement can barely rally the nail that holds it up on the wall. Skip the mission and vision statements.

What we all need is a Battle Cry – something to jump out of bed for; something to be excited about; some reason to show up.

We all want to make a difference, to be significant, to know that our work is important. We need a reason to rally. The Battle Cry gives us that reason to rally.

The Inches Count

"Life is just a game of inches. Inch by inch, play by play. The inches we need are everywhere around us. When we add up all those inches, that's gonna make the difference between winning and losing, between living and dying. That's what living is, the six inches in front of your face."

extracted from Al Pacino's speech as football coach Tony D'Amato in the movie Any Given Sunday

Inches count!

- Acknowledging an employee's effort in spite of a disappointment
- Pausing for patience with the irritating customer service rep
- Chatting with a stranger in line at Starbucks
- Asking questions and being interested in a friend's experience
- Reflecting on what worked and didn't work in yesterday's meeting
- Editing the snarly comment before it leaves your lips or your outbox
- Using recycled bags, returning the shopping cart, saying thank you

Resolutions seem daunting because they ignore the inches. We make grandiose declarations about how we are going to be different people in the new year, but we forget to focus on the six inches in front of our face.

The reality is that we evolve in inches. Our team advances in inches. Our business is won in inches.

It's only through inches that we successfully – but gradually – change and develop into a better version of ourself.

IN A FLASH!

What If We Were Evaluated Only By Our Passion?

One of my favorite movie lines can be heard at the end of the romantic comedy, *Serendipity*:

> "The Greeks didn't write obituaries. They only asked one question after a man died: 'Did he have passion?'"
>
>> * (This is partially true and partially Hollywood. The founders of Cyrenaic (435–356 BC) held this philosophy and they were Greek. But this practice was not true of all Greeks.)

What if we were evaluated only by our passion?

- Would we spend our time differently at home and at the office?
- How would we have to act and behave if passion was a requirement of our job?
- Would we still prioritize our emails and altercations, or our impact and contributions?
- Would we focus more on the output we deliver or the outcome we influence?

If passion were revered and valued at work, would we add it as a leadership competency and evaluate it during the annual performance review: "So Bob, how should we rate your passion this year?"

... and perhaps reinvent the exit interview: "So Bob, did you have passion while you worked at our company?"

So what is passion? Intense enthusiasm, energy, and tenacity for something that excites us. Typically it manifests as:

- Unquenchable desire and devotion
- An internal drive regardless of circumstances
- Dogged determination to make a difference
- Intrepid risk-taking in spite of doubters, naysayers, critics, and judges
- Obsession with improving: self, others, processes, products, profits
- Courage to challenge mediocrity, complacency, and the status quo

But what should do we do if we would fail the Greek's obituary-test today?

Start creating passion... in moments. Soon enough, the moments will add up to define a passionate life. And even the Greeks won't need to write an obituary about us!

Why We Should Listen to Xerox CEO Ursula Burns' Mom

Where you are is not who you are.

Ursula's mom preached these words to her daughter while raising her in a tough, drug-infested ghetto in New York City's Lower East Side. She lectured Ursula about education and hard work being the way up and out of the ghetto.

Ursula Burns recently retired as CEO of Xerox Corporation, a career she started in 1980 as an intern after completing a Master's degree in mechanical engineering. She became the first female African-American CEO of a Fortune 500 company.

What power did Ursula's mom give her? The conviction that our circumstances do not define us ...unless we let them.

We can apply this wisdom to any circumstance:

- What you did is not who you are. A mistake, an error, a bad decision does not define you. You have the power to learn a lesson and act differently going forward.

- What you said is not who you are. A misspoken word, a short temper, a negative moment does not define you. You have the power to apologize and speak differently going forward.

- What you are called is not who you are. Your title does not define you. You have the power to contribute and make a difference regardless of what your business card says.

Ursula's mom taught Ursula to write a different story for herself instead of following the one dictated by her circumstances.

Look for the Experience of Being Alive vs. the Meaning of Life

Author Joseph Campbell astutely observed "I don't believe people are looking for the meaning of life as much as they are looking for the experience of being alive."

As we celebrated my mom's 75th birthday recently, it occurred to me that she has been on a lifelong quest for the experience of being alive:

- When I was growing up, my mom constantly adopted new hobbies: sewing, painting, crocheting, basket weaving, antique collecting
- When she wanted to earn more money, she became a real estate agent and then the managing broker
- When my sister needed a kidney transplant, my mom donated hers without hesitation
- And she won't walk by someone homeless without offering food or money
- After being widowed, she traveled to China alone
- Upon her return, she tried Match.com
- And then at 70 she walked down the aisle again (including a bachelorette party!)
- She once pulled an all-nighter with me for the best seats at the Macy's Day Parade
- After the election, she attended the March on Washington
- Last year she biked Iowa with me
- Last month she started doing yoga
- Last week she tried OrangeTheory Fitness
- And for 40 years she has done it all in long red nails

I can synthesize her strategies to "experience being alive" as follows:

1. Keep perspective ("What's the worst that can happen?")
2. Say "yes!" first; figure out the how later
3. Always have a ticket to the next adventure
4. Make others feel important
5. Go out of your way to help people (Her agents still reflect, "No matter how busy your mom was, she always made time for me.")

While my mom doesn't talk about the meaning of life, she never passes up an opportunity to experience something new or to make a difference for someone else.

Do You Have a Battle Cry Like My Hertz Driver?

A Battle Cry is what we shout as we run onto the proverbial battle field in pursuit of victory!

- William Wallace in the movie *Braveheart*: *They may take our land but they'll never take our freedom!*
- JFK: *We shall pay any price to assure the survival and the success of liberty.*
- Starbucks: *We are inspiring and nurturing the human spirit one person, one cup, one neighborhood at a time.*
- US Marines Corps: *Semper Fidelis* (Always Faithful or Always Loyal)
- Crawford, my Hertz Rental car driver at Orlando airport: *I save marriages.*

Wait! What? Crawford explained, "Dragging all of that luggage and children can test any relationship, especially in the rain. I am in charge of personally driving families who need help getting to the terminal after dropping off their cars. On the way, I talk to them, calm them down, and alleviate their frustrations. I've saved numerous marriages."

We ask ourselves every day to come to work, to be all in, to give a piece of our lives to an organization. We need to show up because we believe ...with our heart and soul.

But people don't believe in to do-lists, monthly goals, or quarterly quotas. We merely tolerate those. We believe in a purpose - the why behind our work - the reason for the lists, goals, and quotas.

Without a Battle Cry, setting goals and generating lists become rote exercises. But a Battle Cry guides our actions and reinforces the fight. And it's not about the money. Money becomes the focus when we lack purpose and passion.

To identify your own Battle Cry, ask yourself:

- what do you love about your job?
- what difference does your work make to others (on your team, in your organization, with your customers, in the community)?

As Crawford dropped me at the terminal, he reflected, "I love my job. I love Hertz." That's the power of the Battle Cry!

Chapter 8

CHANGE

Is It Time for a New Normal?

When normal feels too normal, it might be time for a New Normal.

As I wrote holiday cards to my family, friends, and colleagues one year, I was struck by how many people in my life had courageously created (or endured) a "New Normal" that year.

Some announced new roles or retirements, others changed jobs or addresses, some had children, others sent children off to college, some decided to get married, while others decided to get unmarried.

It takes courage to make change happen. And it's courage that fuels our resilience after change happens to us.

The reality is that we cannot be stuck and in action at the same time. A New Normal forces us to get unstuck.

I've moved to the West coast and then to the East. I've changed jobs. I've changed careers. I've lost a parent. I got married. I embraced step-kids. I bought a house. I got a dog. And then I adopted another dog.

Each experience forced me to get uncomfortable, alter the cadence of my life, and move forward without knowing exactly how it would turn out.

Soon, each experience became my New Normal.

Is Success on the Other Side of Fear?

By January 31, 33% of people abandon their New Year's resolutions. And by June, 77% of people forget they ever had resolutions. Which might explain why less than half the population even bothers to set resolutions each year.

Some experts argue that failure is inevitable because our resolutions are too lofty, too foggy, too easy, or too hard. Other research suggests that we are too busy to stay committed, we suffer from decision fatigue, we don't plan our goals, and we don't have anyone to support us.

What if the only thing standing in our way is fear?

"Everything you've ever wanted is on the other side of fear." (George Adair)

But what are we afraid of?
- Failing (being part of the 77% of resolution quitters!)
- Succeeding (and then having to sustain success all year)
- Judgment and Criticism (by those not changing or improving)
- Disappointment (what if the change is not as great as anticipated?)
- Comparison (what if our resolution is not as ambitious as other people's?)
- Hard Work (don't we already work hard enough?)
- Being Uncomfortable (there's a reason for remote controls and drive-thrus)
- Change (we've finally figured things out so why endure change?)
- Lack of Aspiration (what if we don't even know what we want?)

By acknowledging our fears first, we can walk to the other side of them and then employ all the sage, habit-changing, goal-achieving advice and strategies:
- Write goals down
- Put them in the positive
- Share them with others
- Get a buddy for support
- Anchor a new habit to another habit
- Execute a goal in chunks
- Work on them early each day

We don't need another holiday ritual to make us feel inadequate. We just need to face our fears before they sabotage our success.

Six Seconds Could Change Your Life

I hit someone in third grade. Not a punch. Just a slap on the back, angry about a game I wanted that my classmate wouldn't share. Infuriated by her bratty "No!", I reacted. I was young, immature, and emotionally unintelligent. Fortunately, our teacher wasn't.

Today, my hands don't strike, but my words can. Out of frustration, anger, or defensiveness, I can easily react instead of respond.

Emotional intelligence lies in the moments after an altercation – a skill that can fundamentally improve our leadership and our lives. So I'm learning to pause in those moments.

The 6-Second Rule: Science has determined that emotions are actually electrochemical signals coursing through the brain and body delivering messages that focus our energy and attention, and motivate us to act.

But when we are upset, a burst of these chemicals floods our brain and body, hindering our ability to think clearly or intelligently, and indulging our emotionally unintelligent reactions. Research shows that it takes:

- 6 seconds for those chemicals to get absorbed back into the body
- 6 seconds for us to become objective about the feelings we're feeling
- 6 seconds for us to generate compassion instead

And according to researchers, if we feel an emotion longer than 6 seconds we are – in some ways – choosing to recreate and refuel those feelings.

So how do we create a 6-second habit?

1. Talk about it
2. Use a timer
3. Post visual reminders (ex: post-it notes!)
4. Notice others using it (or not)
5. Pay attention to what triggers those emotions
6. Keep a journal
7. Create an intentional diversion (like singing the alphabet or whistling)
8. Start counting

Six seconds to halt regrettable anger. Six seconds to shift to empathy.
Six seconds to be a better boss, partner, friend, and human being.

Stop Saying I'm So Busy! (and Reclaim Your Sanity!)

We are constantly deluged with an unmanageable amount of information screaming for our attention. Each day sees:

- 269 billion new email messages
- 8 trillion new text messages
- 500 million new tweets

It's not surprising that we get overwhelmed and overpowered by information. Defensively, we utter the phrase, "I'm so busy" like a salutation, "Good morning! I'm so busy!"

So what can we do to stop drowning?

1. Identify our essentials
2. Consume only the information that contributes to those essentials

Without vigilantly deploying these filters, any information can seem intriguing, interesting, or important.

To identify essentials:

"Essential" gets defined by our aspirations, our goals, our commitments, our vision, and our Battle Cry. We need to ask, "What are my aspirations [goals, commitments, vision, Battle Cry for my career, my family, my heath, my finances, and my life?"

To determine what information is important:

Pause to evaluate: "Does this information [email, text, tweet, data, Yahoo story, LinkedIn announcement, Facebook update, YouTube cat video] I'm about to consume contribute to or contaminate one of my aspirations?" ("Contaminate" is any distraction, derailment, or sabotage.)

If the information does not help us move toward that which is important to us (our aspirations!), we need to: resist it, trash it, return it, or ignore it.

The only way to survive the deluge is by taking back our power over the information. When we don't use filters, we don't have control. And then we helplessly grouse, "I'm so busy!"

We can do better than that...

IN A FLASH!

Chapter 9

RESILIENCE

Why the Cubs Made It To the World Series... Finally

After 71 years, the Chicago Cubs are in the World Series again.

What took so long? The Cubs (and fans!) have ingeniously blamed everyone but themselves since 1945.

The Billy Goat Curse: At the 1945 World Series, Billy Sianis brought his goat to watch the Cubs play Game 4. He was ejected from the stadium because the goat smelled. Furious, he placed a hex on the Cubs that they'd lose the game and never return to the World Series. They've blamed the goat ever since.

The Black Cat Curse: In the 1969 playoffs, a black cat strolled past the dugout. The Cubs fell apart, blowing their 9-game lead. They blamed the cat.

The Gatorade Glove: In the 1984 playoffs, an easy-to-field grounder rolled between the legs of Cubs first baseman. He blamed his teammate who spilled Gatorade on his glove in the dugout. The team unraveled again and lost.

The Steve Bartman Incident: In the 2003 playoffs, Steve Bartman sat in the first row of the left field stands, leaned over the wall, and deflected the fly ball that the Cubs outfielder was jumping up to catch. The Cubs subsequently crumbled missing the World Series again. The team (and the entire city of Chicago) immediately blamed it all on Bartman.

And then in 2015, Coach Joe Maddon arrived.

Maddon immediately diagnosed the real Cubs curse: the culture. Without placating the team or mincing words, he proposed a novel idea: they are each solely responsible for their own successes and failures. He was not interested in indulging in any conversation about a goat, a black cat, Gatorade, or Steve Bartman.

He underscored this reality check with his now-famous pep-talk: "Just try not to suck."

And suddenly the Cubs were in the 2016 World Series. They got the message!

When we want to play a new game, we need a new conversation.

Embracing Fiascos and Flops

Bad events are stronger than good ones.

Research shows that we learn from and use negative information far more than positive information when making decisions.

Negative events have a greater impact on us than positive ones. Negative events are more memorable. An embarrassing moment, losing a friend, getting fired, receiving criticism, an altercation with a stranger. We are more motivated to avoid these bad situations than we are to pursue good ones.

It would make sense to focus on our failures to avoid replicating them. But our ego gets in the way of allowing our errors to serve as teaching tools. Instead, we point to bad luck, unfortunate timing, or external circumstances to excuse our gaffes: the weather, the traffic, the sabotaging colleagues, the jerk in the store, our manager's poor judgment, the short-sited client.

And while society has convinced us to study successful people through books, magazines, speakers, and movies; the reality is that success is hard to replicate. There are too many factors involved.

Failure, however, can easily be replicated. So let's focus on others' failures, mistakes, bloopers, errors, and missteps so we don't replicate them:
- When engaging with a Mentor, ask about their mistakes and lessons learned
- When talking with anyone about their success, ask about what didn't work
- When reading about successful people in books and magazines, focus on their errors and blunders
- When in awe of role models, notice their miscalculations and oversights
- Keep a list of failures, fiascos, and flops – yours and other people's,
- Then study the list regularly

Warren Buffet's business partner, Charles Munger, keeps an inanities list and a file of foolishness filled with other people's missteps, errors, and bad judgment. He studies it to ensure he doesn't replicate them.

Create your own Fiascos and Flops List and reference it before making decisions. When everyone else is trying to parrot the successful, you'll be busy generating your own success.

Your But Needs a Break

"Yes, but..." has become our knee-jerk reaction.

When someone suggests an idea, we often respond with, "Yes, but..."

Of course we do! We are high-functioning, successful problem-solvers, masterful at identifying issues and objections. That's our job!

And, it's the aftereffect of "but" that betrays us. Our "but" discredits the suggestion, which in turn disrespects the other person.

Whereas, "AND" builds on the suggestion, and therefore strengthens the partnership with the other person in the conversation.

By using "AND" to introduce the concern or objection, we're preserving, and most importantly welcoming, conversation, exploration, positivity, and possibility.

Here's how it works. In emails and in discussions, pause to respond to an idea, suggestion, or recommendation by employing "yes AND..." (even if it's screaming for a "but!")

- Other person: "I want to offer the client a free workshop."
- Us: "Yes, that would be great ...AND, I think the client would value it more if they paid for it."

Granted, "Yes, AND" requires intentionality and practice, AND the impact on communication, relationships, and trust justifies the extra effort.

Why We Need To Stop Saga-Sharing

Legendary football coach Lou Holtz once said, "Never tell your problems to anyone. 20% don't care and the other 80% are glad you have them."

So why do it? What do we hope to gain from bemoaning problems and doling out drama? Perhaps sympathy, pity, support, or even commiseration.

But here's why we need to stop Saga-Sharing:

- Negativity breeds negativity (in ourselves and others)
- Every time we share the problem, we relive it
- There's no room for reflection, learning, progress, or solutions

And the biggest reason: to be an influential, inspiring leader, we need to focus our attention on others. To do so, we must step out of our world and into theirs. We can't do that when we're busy lamenting our own problems.

So what should we do when other people start Saga-Sharing? Help them shift their focus to solutions:

- Listen
- Empathize: "That sounds awful."
- Ask: "How can I help here?"

By not getting caught in a web of grousing and grumbling, we open the door to growth, resilience, and possibility – ours and theirs.

Would You Believe in Victory with 10 Seconds Left?

At halftime the Minnesota Vikings were up 17–0 and feeling confident they would win the NFC Championship game against the New Orleans Saints.

But the Saints came back with a vengeance, scoring throughout the second half. With less than a minute to go, the Saints scored a field goal that seemed to secure their win.

There was no way the Vikings were coming back. They were 71 yards away from the end zone with 10 seconds left on the clock. Vikings fans were already mourning. Even the Saints started celebrating their inevitable victory.

But the Vikings never gave up. They played those last 10 seconds with perseverance and determination. They made every second count.

The quarterback Case Keenum threw the football to wide receiver Stefon Diggs who jumped to catch it, averted being tackled, caught himself when he lost his balance, and sprinted 61 yards for the game-winning touchdown!

It was incredible! But it wasn't a miracle. It was possibility and intentionality (and talent!) in action.

How can we help our teams believe in possibility and act with intention to the very last second?

- **Focus Don't Flounder:** The players ruthlessly battled together toward the same goal.
- **Coach Don't Rescue:** The Vikings coach did not come running onto the field to grab the football and save the game.
- **Praise Don't Persecute:** It is easy (and habitual) for the rest of us to judge and criticize from the sidelines.
- **Strategize Don't Victimize:** Nobody can play the victim and rouse the remarkable simultaneously.
- **Cheer Don't Berate:** Yelling and screaming doesn't work to inspire dogs, babies, or team members.

When you're racing the clock on a deadline, a project, or a race... use your words and actions to strengthen people's belief in themselves and commitment to victory.

Chapter 10

CONNECTING

Why St. Paul's Cathedral Banned Photos

"No Photos Allowed!" read signs throughout St. Paul's Cathedral in London.

Curious, I asked, "Why?"

A curator explained, "The tour guides got frustrated because people were too busy taking pictures and not paying attention."

Essentially, they were tired of competing with smartphones!

The draconian restriction worked. The church was scattered with enrapt tourists intently listening to the guides.

Named the "iPhone Effect," psychologists have discovered that the mere presence of a smartphone (even if not being used) inhibits conversation.

Why? Because the smartphone divides our attention between the proximate and the possible – between the person in front of us and the world of people potentially calling, texting, tweeting, and posting.

When our smartphone is on the table or in our hands, the other person knows they are competing for our attention, and this distract-ability diminishes the quality of our interaction.

- The conversation remains shallow, careening instead of flowing.
- Consequently, people restrict their responses.
- And this decreases our empathy.

Ironically, being constantly connected is interfering with our connections.

Because leading intentionally depends on these connections, our rapt attention and empathy are essential. And so our challenge: to deliberately disconnect.

Maybe we need to occasionally post our own sign: No Smartphones Allowed.

Are you a Wayfinder? (Human Connection is Still Valuable)

The Metropolitan Transportation Agency spent years automating the NYC subway operations: vending machines, mapping apps, and electronic fare payment. All of it obviating the need for human interaction to ride the subway.

And then last week they deployed a crew of "Wayfinders" – customer service ambassadors positioned at subway stations to greet people, answer questions, help anyone hurt or sick, and offer route advice.

Why? Wayfinders are able to serve people individually, in ways technology falls short.

A similar "Wayfinder" experience occurred on my recent JetBlue flight. Waiting at the gate, everyone knew the flight was delayed. We saw it on the airport monitors; we received text updates on our phones. Aggravations were simmering, and the automated updates failed to placate.

And then suddenly Captain Jerry came out to the gate area. He shared inside information about why the inbound flight was delayed. He described the conditions that we could expect once we got airborne; he even interacted with us about the football game erupting on the televisions.

And as he walked back onto the plane to prepare the cockpit, he playfully said, "If you all drink responsibly, I promise to drive responsibly!" The crowd loved him! Our frustrations were instantly abated.

We are surrounded by automation, while starved for human connection.

The subway isn't less crowded or more efficient. My flight didn't take off on time. But the Wayfinders certainly diffuse our irritation, and that makes the difference.

Where are you depending on technology or automation at the expense of a human connection? Even a phone call instead of an email or a text could shift the experience for you and another.

I've seen these Wayfinders in action – they are having a lot more fun than Alexa or Siri, and as a result, so do we.

Connect in Inches. Engage in Yards

Each day we interact with a myriad of people, exchanging pleasantries as we pass. "How are you?" How was your weekend?" "What's new?" "How was school today?"

And in each interaction, as we are asking, we anticipate their one-word answers: "Good" "Great" "Nothing" "Fine."

1-inch questions yield 1-inch answers. This is vital to our survival, ensuring we connect with cordiality, but without getting stuck in conversation. One-inch questions allow us to ask without stopping, ask while half-listening, ask while multi-tasking, all while moving through the day.

But to engage with others, we must evolve the 1-inch question into a Yardstick question:

- Really? What was that like?
- What did you learn?
- What was your experience?
- Anything surprise you?
- Interesting. Tell me more.

Yardstick questions force us to pause for a person, intentionally making the world revolve around them. Suddenly, we are listening as if our relationship depends on it, and when it's authentic, they feel it. To ask a Yardstick question, we naturally become curious, eager, and present – because we truly don't know the answers.

Yardstick questions reveal volumes about us. Yardstick answers reveal volumes about them. And the result is transformative, not just transactional.

- We care.
- They trust.
- They share.
- We trust.
- They care.

When we need to get by someone, we ask 1-inch questions. When we need to get through someone, we ask Yardstick questions. 1-inch questions create transactional connections. Yardstick questions create transformational engagement.

Are You Interesting or Interested?

We have great stories, ideas, and perspectives – all leaders do. And we tend to share (and over-share) them.

Why? To educate, espouse, entertain, connect, and sometimes impress people.

But when we devour the stage, we forget that others covertly yearn for us to want to hear their stories, ideas, and perspectives.

Our simple invitation "What's your experience?" "What's your story?" "What do you think?" often reveals a treasure-trove.

For some it takes courage to share. They'll do so only if they know we are willing to truly listen (and not just biding time to grab the mic).

Why should we listen? Because by being more interested (than interesting) in discovering others' stories, ideas, and perspectives, we actually fuel the essential trust we need to lead.

We are each the most interesting person we know. But to courageously lead, we need to be the most *interested* person we know.

Are you being interesting or interested?

Are You a Spotlight Stealer?

I've been hooked on Katie Couric podcasts lately. What I love most about Katie is her rabid curiosity. She is masterful at shining the spotlight on others. And when someone shares an experience similar to hers, she never steals the spotlight with, "That happened to me too. Let me tell you my experience..."

We are guilty of Spotlight Stealing when someone tells us their story and we jump in with our own story.

We don't do it maliciously, and (typically) we don't intend to be rude. We actually share our just-like-me stories because humans connect based on similarities. We pivot to our story – which is just like theirs – because we want to bond.

But in doing so, we inadvertently steal the spotlight. We grab the microphone. We push them off the stage.

To truly develop a connection with someone, we need to keep the spotlight on them until the bulb flickers and fades. How?

- Be genuinely interested and curious
- Use 1-inch and yardstick questions
- Ask follow-up questions
- Eliminate or mitigate distractions (Katie Couric never checks FaceBook in an interview!)
- Listen like you're on assignment

It takes a conscious effort not to steal the spotlight, but the boon to the relationship is worth it:

- They feel listened to and important
- Their trust in us increases
- We connect and bond

And because of that increased trust, they more readily disclose information to us. We gain access to their beliefs, knowledge, and attitudes, thus further strengthening our bond and our ability to make a difference.

Don't worry. We'll get our turn on the stage. But remember, our power to connect and influence lies in letting someone else have the spotlight. Just listen to Katie Couric in action!

Don't Kill the Laugh Track *(Humor Turns Strangers into Supporters)*

A Manager glumly reported to me, "I received feedback from my peers that I use humor too much. So my goal is to eliminate humor."

Whoa! We need humor and here's why... Strangers scare us. The stress of being among strangers actually has a name: "social stress barrier to empathy." Without a relationship, even our peers are considered strangers.

Being among strangers feels dangerous because we fear being judged or criticized. This anxiety blocks our ability to empathize. And without empathy, it's impossible to garner trust – the linchpin of all great relationships!

So we are left with strangers when we really need supporters.

Role of laughter: Research shows that laughter and play actually blocks the social stress anxiety, and this allows us to connect, bond, empathize, and trust.

How? Laughter releases endorphins – the feel-good chemicals in our brain. Endorphins signal that it's safe to connect with others and deepen the relationship.

Not surprisingly laughter is one of the most contagious of our emotions. Even a simple shared moment of humor can release tension and decrease anxiety.

So how can we generate laughter and play?

- Create fun experiences (team-building off-sites, on-sites, lunches, parties)
- Incorporate games into meetings
- Point out the humor in situations (like standing in a long line for a cup of coffee!)
- Self-deprecate with sarcasm
- Share embarrassing moments
- Exchange funny cartoons and YouTube videos
- Tell funny (and appropriate!) jokes

Of course ill-timed, inappropriate, and cruel humor communicates a lack of understanding, empathy, and kindness. But that's about being emotionally intelligent and mindful of situations, not about killing the laugh track.

When we want to convert strangers into supporters, we can deploy humor to easily connect with others.

Relationships Need Weeding

Like a garden, relationship weeds result from neglect.

Upsets, miscommunications, missed expectations, disappointments, frustrations, altercations, and conflict – each a weed that sprouts in our personal and professional relationships.

When relationships are new, weeds are rare. We are too busy making a good impression, establishing trust, creating rapport, becoming a new boss, or being the new team member. In new relationships, we are intentionally vigilant against weeds.

However, when we get comfortable in our relationships, we tend to get lazy. We forget to update our boss; we make a decision without including our team; we fail to follow up on a commitment; we cancel meetings or show up late; we neglect to set expectations on an assignment; we tolerate emotional outbursts; we inflict snarly or rude comments.

Like gardeners, we must diligently pull weeds to foster those relationships.

Here's your candid, no B.S., weed-pulling script:
- What's working for you?
- What's not working for you?
- Here's what's working for me...
- Here's what's not working for me...

Example:
- What's working for you? I love this new project
- What's not working for you? I'm not getting the support I need from you.
- Here's what's working for me... I'm excited to see your leadership shine in this new project.
- Here's what's not working for me... I need you to get better at delegating so other work gets done.

As you embark on pulling weeds, a few pointers:
1. Start by identifying a topic, a situation, an issue, a relationship weed to address.

---

2. Emphasize your commitment to the relationship and to the other person's success.

3. Muster your courage. It can be uncomfortable asking for such pointed feedback, but your vulnerability will invite theirs.

4. Prepare for some defensiveness, especially if the neglect has eroded the trust between you. Reaffirm your commitment.

5. Focus on the issue, not the person.

When a relationship matters, weed-whacking doesn't work. You need to intentionally and unabashedly pull the weeds to strengthen the soil that allows the relationship garden to flourish.

Chapter 11

CONFLICT

Is Being Right Getting in the Way of Being in Relationship?

A mom wrote to the "Social Qs" columnist in *The New York Times* about her adult daughter, an actress who stars in many theater productions. Apparently, the daughter gets upset when the mom doesn't bring flowers to every opening night or doesn't compliment every performance.

The mom's side: She's being dramatic. I don't think every performance or production is worthy of flowers or compliments.

Social Qs response: You could be right... and you get to choose. You can be right or you can be in relationship with your daughter.

Brilliant!

"Being right" typically stems from our upset when someone has not met our engagement expectations. As an example, we expect a colleague to get back to us. When he doesn't, we get frustrated or upset. And we justify our upset by being right and making him wrong.

But focusing on being right about the situation makes it difficult to improve the process and move forward in our relationship with our colleague.

Why? Because "being right" involves criticizing, blaming, and judging. And no one likes being in a relationship feeling criticized, blamed, and judged. It weakens the relationship's foundation of trust.

Kenneth Ziegler, CEO of Logicworks, gets it. He works with, in his words, incredibly intelligent, whimsical personalities who often engage like a dysfunctional family.

But Ziegler says his job is to make people successful. So he exercises patience for the varying degrees of dysfunction, as long as people follow the rules and don't act like they're more important than the company or their team.

Ziegler understands that to help people be successful, he needs to be in relationship with them. Making people wrong about how they function and engage would threaten those relationships and sabotage his commitment.

Joy at work and in life depends on our relationships. Suddenly, "being right" seems so sophomoric.

Lower Your Expectations; Raise Your Aspirations

Lower your expectations. I first heard this advice at RAGBRAI, the annual bike ride across Iowa held the last week of July since 1973.

When my friends and I arrived at camp to start the adventure, the head of our outfitter, Pork Belly Ventures, welcomed us with the following:

> *"This is going to be a great week. But here's the reality: it's hot; you're sleeping in a tent; and you're riding with 10,000 cyclists into towns built for 400 residents. Just lower your expectations."*

Brilliant. Most employed advice of the week. Whenever anything was about to cause an upset (like the mid-week downpour and tent-flooding), we would look at each other and say, "Lower your expectations."

When our expectations are high, we easily get disappointed, angry, and upset. In fact, conflict is merely the result of missed expectations. One person's expectations are higher than another person's. That gap produces the conflict.

Here's how to apply the advice from RAGBRAI:

- We can have high expectations of things we manage: time, money, budgets, deadlines, and projects.
- We get in trouble when we place high expectations on things we do not manage and therefore cannot control: weather, traffic, airlines, and people.

Expectations are things to be managed. People are not.

So what should we do with those high expectations we have been dumping on people? Exchange those expectations for aspirations.

We influence aspirations. We control expectations.

New Rules:

- If you cannot control it, then lower your expectations around it.
- Exchange those high expectations of people with high aspirations for people.
- Then influence the success of those aspirations by relentlessly leading and contributing.
- Lower your expectations. Raise your aspirations.

Running Backs and Defensive Linebackers

Just like on the football field, the workforce is fraught with Running Backs and Defensive Linebackers.

Running Backs catch new ideas and help us run them to the end zone, navigating obstacles in their path.

Defensive Linebackers block us from easily reaching the goal with their naysaying (lots of no-can-do talk) and no-doing (lots of can-do talk, but no action).

Buy why? Why block good ideas? Fear, concern, or confusion.

- Why didn't I think of that idea? Does this mean that I'm not needed anymore?
- Will I get in trouble if this goes through and fails?
- I don't get it and I've got enough I'm already trying to figure out

The secret to working with Defensive Linebackers: purposeful perception. We need to respond not react, discern the real issue, and consider the view from their sidewalk.

Ask yourself:

- What's really going on - what's their fear, concern, or confusion?
- How can I address it?
- How can I help them win when I win?

And while it's easy to judge others, we must consider when new ideas come to us, are *we* being the Running Back or the Defensive Linebacker?

Stop Having Difficult Conversations

Jane's boss: Jane, you keep avoiding that difficult conversation you need to have with your employee.

Jane: Fine. I'll do it. I'll be mean.

Whoa! She just framed the difficult conversation in a very disempowering way.

No wonder we habitually avoid difficult/crucial/confronting conversations – our focus is on the other person's judgment or reaction!

- Will they think I'm rude, unkind, unfair, or mean?
- Will they get defensive or upset?

What Jane and the rest of us difficult-conversation-avoiders need is a new frame on a ubiquitous challenge.

Conversations are:

- difficult when we make it about their judgment or reaction
- valuable when we make it about their success

When we shift the focus from their reaction/judgment to our intention to support their success, these conversations become the gateway to our contributions.

Being committed to their success allows us to welcome (not avoid) the conversation that will contribute to that success:

"Let's have a commitment conversation. As your boss, I am committed to your success. However, based on the goals you've shared with me, the behavior I'm observing is not serving your success."

Stop having difficult conversations and start having commitment conversations.

Beware of "No Creep"

Everyone has the power to say No. (Very few have the power to say Yes.)

And when lots of people are flexing their power, No starts creeping into interactions.

Here's what No Creep sounds like:

- That won't work.
- That's not our policy.
- We can't do it that way.
- You need to follow the process.
- There is not enough time. I'm too busy.
- We need another meeting before we can take action.
- You need more approvals on this before you can move forward.

No Creep is destructive. People stop uniting for the sake of the customer and the success of the company. The result? Exhausting and debilitating internal dogfights.

No Creep obstructs solutions. People stop looking for solutions – too busy out-No'ing each other. And the lack of solutions breeds embittered employees, frustrated customers, and agonizing sales.

Want to outrival your competitors? Dethrone the power to just say No. Reward the power to find solutions. Declare "No, but..." as the new norm ("No, but here's what we could do...")

And block No Creep with these questions:

- How could we make that work?
- What do we need to do to move this forward?
- How can we improve this process?
- How can I help you?
- How can we get the customer what they need and want?
- What's our objective? How can we get there?
- How can we all win?

What are you doing to enervate the power of No and invigorate the power of solutions?

Confront Don't Cower, Incite Don't Ignore

Just when we thought bullying was the most injurious, new research reveals that ignoring is actually worse.

This reality can be explained by our basic human needs:

- to be recognized and accepted
- to interact, connect, and belong
- to matter

When we fight, at least we are interacting and connecting – the altercation serves as evidence that the people in it actually exist.

But when we ignore someone, we reject, banish, and ostracize them – confirming their fear of irrelevance. As a result, ignoring easily leads to feelings of humiliation, helplessness, insecurity, and a motivation to quit. And this transpires even when our actions are not intentionally ignoring, but merely a reflection of our own lack of courage or inability to confront.

Ignoring (intentionally or unintentionally) can take many forms:

- not responding to texts, emails, or calls
- not inviting or including someone
- not hearing (or pretending not to hear) a question/comment
- silent treatment

As with all experiences, ostracism is the in the eye of the sufferer, not the culprit. Our own intent, perception, or projected response becomes insignificant.

Short of coddling everyone on our team, what should we do? Help people matter:

- respond and recognize
- include and interact
- argue and altercate
- confront and clarify
- dig in and empathize
- and communicate when we can't

It takes arrogance or cowardice to ignore someone. But it takes courage to respect their contribution, even if we dislike it, them, or the situation. Ultimately, we are better leaders when we confront instead of cower, and include instead of ignore.

Chapter 12

COMMUNICATIONS

Do You Speak in Bullets?

People are distracted.

- They multi-task.
- They skim.
- They defer to emoticons, texts, and pictures.
- They are inundated with sound bites, ads, alerts, and scrolling news blasts.

Research shows that the human attention span has dropped to 8 seconds – even shorter than goldfish!

If we want to lead even without a title, we need to capture attention, command respect, and cement our leadership presence. We need to speak in bullets.

To speak in bullets:

- be brief
- highlight important points
- skip the backstory
- use metaphors to captivate, bolster comprehension, and increase retention

If and when your audience wants more information, they'll ask for it.

Most people communicate unintentionally – they process out loud.

But we can help people develop this essential leadership skill, thereby increasing their efficiency, effectiveness, and impact.

How? Start by teaching people how to speak in bullets.

- Give them a time limit: "I want to hear what you have to say, and I only have two minutes."
- Interrupt their meandering with, "I'm going to interrupt you."
- Remind people: "I don't need the back story yet."
- Then ask, "What's the question?"
- or "What is the key information I need to know?"
- or "Where do you need the most help?"

If we want to be seen as a leader and develop other leaders, we need to start with intentional speaking and purposeful listening. Fewer adjectives, more verbs.

Unless I'm Willing to Be Changed by You, I'm Not Really Listening

I've been inhaling Alan Alda's book, *If I Understood You, Would I Have This Look on My Face?* Besides having an irreverent title, it's a valuable book on relating and communicating. In it Alan Alda proposes two game-changing concepts to help us bridge the ever-increasing chasm between people who attempt to communicate with each other:

1. It's not your job to understand me.

Essentially, if I'm communicating information, I am responsible for making sure you understand it. If I tell you something without ensuring that you got it (received it and understood it), then I didn't really communicate.

Bottom line... I am 100% responsible for my communications.

As such, I need to ensure that...

- I am not mumbling or talking too fast
- I write clearly and without assumptions
- I am able to synthesize information (remember: start with bullets!)
- You have the requisite context for the topic
- You understand any lingo, jargon, or acronyms I choose to use
- My email, text, IM, memo, tweet, or letter actually made it to you

As the speaker, it is my job to make sure you follow. It is not your job to catch up.

2. Unless I'm willing to be changed by you, I'm probably not really listening.

Real communication does not occur if I'm simply waiting for my turn to talk. I need to approach the conversation like an improv exercise.

This requires me to:
- Suspend what I already know about the topic
- Let go of what I expect to happen in our exchange
- Stay present (not mind-wander or text)
- Be eager to discover where you take the conversation with your contribution

Ultimately, we get to create conversation together. Imagine the shift in discourse at work and in life if we approached each other with these two simple, yet powerful principles of communication.

Listen to their Listening (or Just Stop Speaking)

In an old episode of the television comedy *Will & Grace*, narcissistic Karen is scanning the room while talking with her friends at a cocktail party. Suddenly she exclaims, "Better people! Gotta go!"

While we could blame the Karens of the world for being incredibly rude, we are always responsible for our own communication.

And so we need to listen to their listening. When we listen to people, we listen to their words. When we listen to people's listening, we are listening for what they are not saying, such as:

- *I am distracted*
- *I am bored*
- *I am confused*
- *I am stressed or overwhelmed*
- *I am unsure or insecure*
- *I don't agree with you*

When we speak, we are focused on our words. When we listen to their listening, we are focused on their *experience* of our words.

Notice the following:

- Eye contact: where are they looking?
- Focus: are their eyes glazing, clearly thinking about other things?
- Face: are they smiling, frowning, furrowing their brows, or pursing their lips?
- Body language: are their arms crossed, or are they seeking an exit?
- Responses: do their comments or answers match the conversation or questions?
- Distractions: are they typing on a keyboard or sucked into a screen?

And when our listening reveals that they are not listening, we can:

1. Stop talking: silence can be very loud
2. Ask a question: "What's your perspective? What do you think?"
3. Acknowledge the distraction: "Do you need to take that call/text?"
4. Reschedule the conversation: "This doesn't seem to be a good time; shall we reschedule?"

If we want to be better bosses, parents, friends, neighbors, and even strangers, we need to shift the spotlight from our stage to theirs by intentionally listening to their listening.

Do You Listen With Thunder or Lightning?

"That's crazy! Why are you doing that!?" my friend challenged. *Lightning!*

"Wow! That's amazing. What was that like?" my other friend appreciated. *Thunder!*

Thunder claps. Lightning strikes.

- When we listen with thunder, we clap with acknowledgement, recognition, interest, and support.
- When we listen with lightning, we strike from defensiveness or judgment.

Why? When we listen with lightning, we take the focus off of the other person and we make it about us.

We start to wonder...

- What does that person's comment mean about me?
- If that person is growing, does that mean I'm shrinking?
- If that person has great news, does mine pale in comparison?
- If that person makes a bold decision or holds a strong opinion, does that question my decision or opinion?

But when we listen with thunder, we engage with a steadfast focus on the other person. We are cognizant that acknowledging their success, their growth, their decision, and their opinion bears no reflection on our own.

And that takes awareness, intentionality, and courage.

If we are committed to serving the success of others, we need to listen with more thunder and less lightning.

Bring a Highlighter to Conversations that Matter

Our people vigilantly gauge our reactions. They examine our words and our actions. They scrutinize the tone of our voice, the furrow of our brows, the subtext of our emails.

What are they looking for? Our approval. (We all have an intrinsic need to feel valued and appreciated.)

At the risk of doling out daily blue ribbons, how can we acknowledge others in a way that makes a difference?

Bring a highlighter to the conversations that matter.

We use highlighters to accentuate key points in a book. We can use highlighters to accentuate key points in a conversation.

How?

- Comment on the effort a person made
- Observe a learning they had
- Reflect on an improved process they implemented
- Remark on progress they've made

The key to effective highlighting is to listen for impact and make it specific. Example: "I am impressed by what a difference your new approach made during that sales call."

Not only will people feel acknowledged, they will repeat whatever we highlight. Our acknowledgement triggers their dopamine – the highly addictive feel-good chemical in the brain.

How can we remember to do this regularly? Make highlighting a habit!

- Add it to the end of every agenda
- Post a note on the computer or phone
- Add it to a daily to-do list
- Tie it like a ribbon to the end of every conversation

When we serve people's success, it is our responsibility to highlight the efforts they make in an attempt to serve our success.

Forget the Golden Rule! Adopt the Titanium Rule to Communicate

The Golden Rule is probably the worst advice we can follow when communicating with people.

"Do unto others as you would have them do unto you" causes us to communicate with others as we want them to communicate with us.

For example:
- I want skim-able emails with bullets, so I send skim-able emails with bullets
- I talk fast, and I expect others to listen fast
- I respond to texts immediately, so I expect others to do the same

My approach to communication works for me, but it's contemptuous to assume it works for everyone. If I email someone who only talks on the phone, we will invariably miscommunicate.

To eliminate frustrations and ensure we connect, we need to follow the Titanium Rule: communicate with others as *they* would like to be communicated to.

Titanium is strong, flexible, and refractory. It's powerful enough to strengthen relationships, while its flexibility allows us to bend when communicating with others to meet their individual needs in any exchange.

And endeavoring to communicate using the Titanium Rule demonstrates our commitment and our respect, while garnering their trust.

What can we do to start adopting the Titanium Rule?
- Notice how others communicate (this informs us of their preferences)
- Ask how they want to receive information (text, email, phone, video, memo, in person)
- Refer to their time zone (don't force them to do the conversion)
- Use acronyms they know
- Provide the context or background information they need
- Use subject lines to personalize (ex: Bob – the agenda you asked for is attached)

Like leading, the Titanium Rule is all about knowing our audience and meeting them where they are.

Know Your Audience

When I grudgingly moved from California to New Jersey a decade ago, I regaled everyone I met with stories about "amazing San Francisco!"

The result? It took me a long time to make friends. Why? I violated an important rule of connecting: *know your audience.*

Whether we are talking with new neighbors, teaching a workshop, exploring an idea with a team, or giving a presentation from the stage, we need to start with "know your audience" not "know your topic."

1. Know who is in the audience (their background and experiences)
2. Understand their communication preferences (do they want stories, bullets, research, experiences, props?)
3. Relate to them (what do you have in common with them?)
4. Consider their reaction to the topic/message (will they be defensive or curious?)
5. Ascertain their priorities (what's important to them?)
6. Determine why your topic is important to them (why are they willing to listen?)
7. Talk about what's important to them (frame your topic/message accordingly)

Some practical ways to "know your audience:"

- Interview people before a meeting/presentation to learn their priorities, preferences, and perspectives (don't just rely on titles and assumptions!)
- Ask questions to involve people and determine what they want to learn about you or the topic
- Be flexible and adapt based on what you discover
- Provide context and backstory (...if they want it)
- Explain jargons and acronyms (...if they need it)
- Observe their listening (notice eye contact, smartphone usage, facial expressions)

- Look around and see where you're at - let the environment inform (ex: people who live in NJ don't want to hear incessantly how great it is to live someplace else!)
- Be patient and curb your defensiveness if they disagree or appear disinterested

To build trust and respect, audiences (of all sizes) want to know that we get them and that what we're saying actually matters to them.

Essentially, people just want to know that we care about their stage before our own.

Chapter 13

COMPASSION

Don't Judge One's Story by the Chapter You Walked In On

Jerk. That's how I described the New Cashier when I left the store. He couldn't help me, didn't try, and was rude.

When I returned the next day, I made a snide comment about the Jerk to my Favorite Cashier who said, "Oh! That's Sam. This is his first job out of college. He's a bit overwhelmed and horribly under-trained, and as a result, he lacks the confidence to engage. I hope he will learn from great customers like you!"

Yikes. Now who's the Jerk?

On the way home, I drove by a sign at a local business that read:

> Don't judge one's story by the chapter you walked in on.

Seriously!? Was that directed at me personally? I had judged Sam's entire story by our 5-minute interaction. I wrote him off as a Jerk.

How many times have I judged other people's entire story based on one exchange? She's thoughtless. He's arrogant. She's mean. He's stupid.

In every interaction, we walk into a chapter of someone's story. And typically we're missing context: we don't know what transpired in that story before we arrived on the scene

> "Don't judge a book by its cover."
> "Don't judge a book by one chapter."

So what can we do? Exactly what my Favorite Cashier suggested: contribute to the chapter.

So here's what I did. On my next visit to the store, I asked Sam about himself and how he's liking his new job. And when he struggled to answer another customer's question, I jumped in to help, mentoring Sam in the process.

When we remember that we are only experiencing one chapter in each person's story, we can approach people with less judgment and more curiosity.

Armed with renewed empathy, patience, and kindness, we can offer to contribute and make a difference.

Don't Boo the Band

My ten-year-old nephew Joaquin is dauntless. He will try any new toy, game, sport, or instrument. He's on the swim team, plays violin in an orchestra, loves basketball, inhales video games, and is learning archery.

And he is perseverant in improving his skills in each new activity.

Recently he was eager to experience Guitar Hero, a video game in which players strum a guitar-shaped game controller and match the notes scrolling on the television screen in time to the music. When the player matches the notes, he scores points and delights the virtual audience in the game. But if the player misses a note, the virtual audience boos instead of cheers.

After playing a while, Joaquin turned with tears in his eyes and said to his mom, "Every time I mess up, my band boos me."

While he was prepared to make mistakes, he wasn't prepared to be boo-ed as he learned the game.

None of us are! When we are in the process of learning and growing, getting boo-ed can quickly crush our spirits.

And yet people regularly boo each other, sometimes inadvertently, sometimes in jest:

- discouraging or dissuading comments
- judging, mocking, or ridiculing
- scoring anonymous surveys unreasonably low
- submitting unkind comments or reviews online
- leaving bad tips

Wait! Don't we need to provide people with feedback to help them learn?

Absolutely! But unkind comments, unreasonably low scores, and bad tips are rarely accompanied by suggestions for improvement. They serve only to dignify the boo-er; they don't serve the learner's growth and development.

When we are committed to contributing to people as they learn and grow, our comments must make *them* feel superior, not us.

Less boos, more woo-hoo's.

Are you a Storyteller or a Storycatcher?

"You just made me feel so important! Thank you for being interested in my life!" Jacqueline, my Uber driver, announced as she dropped me off at DFW airport.

What did I do? Just asked her questions about her adventures as a Texan-from-Louisiana, an insatiable traveler, a wife, a mom, and an Uber driver. Sensing my genuine curiosity and desire to connect, she told me her story, and I caught it.

Now I use every Uber ride to practice my storycatching. It turns a transactional ride into a transformational encounter.

And I've discovered that being interested in other people's stories forces me to:
- listen purposefully
- connect without an agenda
- get over myself
- be empathic
- learn about people, places, and things
- and appreciate others' experiences

And I love storytellers! They entertain, enlighten, teach, and reveal themselves through each story.

But someone has to be there to catch their stories....

So why should we be the Storycatcher?
- We can discover people on a deeper level – how/why they make decisions.
- We might uncover more about issues and situations.
- We demonstrate our concern for and commitment to others.
- We strengthen our patience, empathy, and compassion.
- We are more interesting individuals when we are interested in others.

But being an effective Storycatcher requires authentic curiosity, evoking questions, and deliberate listening.

Start with simple, 1-inch questions:
- How was your weekend?
- Where are you from?
- How long have you been doing this job?

Then draw out the story with follow-up, yardstick questions:

- What was that experience like?
- What was a highlight from your weekend/vacation/situation?
- What did you learn? Anything surprise you?

Catching stories builds empathy and trust, allowing us to step into another's journey and connect as human beings.

Do You Need to Clean Your People Lenses? (ask my friend Lynnae)

"We don't see things the way they are. We see things the way we are."

attributed to author Anais Nin and the Jewish Talmud.

In essence, two people, based on their different perspectives, can have two different points of view on the same topic. (Just watch any news item reported on MSNBC and then on Fox and you'll hear two different sides of that news story.)

Let's evolve this powerful truism to: "We don't see *people* the way they are. We see people the way we are."

Most of our people problems stem from divergent perceptions, which are formed by our:

- beliefs, prejudices, biases
- experiences
- gender, ethnicity, generation
- geography

We then engage with people based on our perceptions – through our own lenses. My best friend, Lynnae, tried teaching me this throughout high school. As we walked down the halls and passed much cooler classmates, I would decry, "She is such a jerk." And Lynnae would respond genuinely, "Well, she's nice to me."

My lenses were blurred by my own teenage insecurities, which created for me a perception that these girls were stuck up and conceited. But Lynnae didn't have those same insecurities muddying her lenses, so her experience of our classmates was different than mine. If only I had cleaned my glasses, I might have graduated with as many friends as Lynnae did!

When we let our lenses get clouded, blurred, or broken, we risk relationships with people. We see people as we are – through the lens of our own biases, beliefs, and past experiences. And then we act as if we are seeing clearly.

The result? Disconnect. Disrespect. Judgment.

If we have any chance of leading people, we have to remember that everyone shows up with their own pair of glasses. We can't clean their lenses, but we can clean (and replace!) our own.

Could the Law of Polarity Make us More Compassionate?

The Law of Polarity states that everything has a polar opposite.

In physics, polarity is a basic feature of the universe. Positive and negative forces are foundational to the structure of every atom.

If everything has a polar opposite, then perhaps...

- a problem cannot exist without a solution
- an opinion cannot exist without an opposing opinion

Maybe the struggle we have lies in our failure to *contemplate* a solution or consider an opposing opinion.

As an example, Peter and Mary work as sales reps at an event company that just implemented a new policy whereby customers will not be charged for cancellations.

Peter is frustrated by the policy. He orders lunches and copies based on reservations. Why should he have to pay for no-shows? And how could he possibly manage his sales with such uncertainty? This policy makes it super easy for people to cancel.

Mary has the polar opposite perspective and approach. Mary is enthusiastic about the policy because of its ability to attract customers. In every sales conversation, she excitedly shares the benefit of working with her company: people can register now to save their seat and cancel any time. This policy makes it super easy for people to commit.

Mary's sales have gone up, while Peter's have gone down. Same policy. Opposing perspectives.

- What if every problem we face actually has a solution that we just haven't yet identified?
- What if every argument has an opposing viewpoint that we just need to ponder?
- What if every negative experience has a positive experience that we just need to discover?

Of course, all of this requires that we suspend our judgment about a policy, situation, or person in favor of contemplation, consideration, and compassion.

IN A FLASH!

Walk to their Fence

Picture a man in his backyard. To talk to his neighbors, he walks to their fence. The man doesn't jump over the fence; he walks to it and stops. Why? Because that's where his neighbors are.

To "walk to their fence" is to meet people where they are.

To do that, we need to know where their fence is:

- Some people enjoy talking on the phone. Others prefer Facebook.
- Some people respond to texts immediately. Others take days to respond.
- Some people greet us with smiles and curiosity. Others are guarded and uninterested.
- Some people are optimistic. Others are pessimistic or melodramatic.

But why can't people connect and engage with us in the same way we connect and engage with them?

These missed interactions are laden with frustration and ripe with personal affronts, which can easily spiral into altercation and alienation.

But I've discovered recently that when I meet people where they are, I remember that it's not about me. And that makes me less critical and more empathetic in my relationships – new and old, personal and professional.

By walking to their fence....

- We don't climb fences to connect, expecting people to applaud our gestures.
- We don't get annoyed when people don't reciprocate and scale fences for us.
- We acknowledge that their fence is as far as they can or will go.
  And that's OK.

Instead of jumping over fences and expecting a celebration, let's learn to walk to their fence and just meet people where they are.

Chapter 14

PERSPECTIVE

Zoom Out! (Advice for the Screen-Obsessed)

I grew up with maps. Big, bulky, beautiful, Rand McNally maps. And a globe. These taught me to look for details while appreciating the big picture.

Today our smartphones have map applications, offering precise, turn-by-turn directions. With only a small screen, we can get to where we're going and never notice what city we're driving through.

But to see the landscape, we need to Zoom Out.

When we're constantly zoomed-in at work and in our lives, we are gripped by small screens and small issues. And our sense of curiosity atrophies in the wake.

We unwittingly neglect what's outside the small screen or the small issue. We read information online without questioning its veracity or source, we stop noticing our surroundings, we become indifferent to the people around us.

And then we miss the meaning... unless we Zoom Out!

What does it mean to Zoom Out?

- Look up and look around
- Consider every party's viewpoint (not just the one side you heard)
- Understand how a project/task fits into the big picture (unsure? ask!)
- Question what's next (think one step ahead of your boss)
- Have an opinion (eliminate "I don't know" from your vernacular)
- Endeavor to improve processes and procedures
- Analyze, think, be curious

Our obsession with screens (literal and figurative) creates our myopia. Being incessantly zoomed-in shortchanges our ability to make a difference, because we lack foresight, discernment, and meaning.

We need to Zoom Out!

As a reminder for myself, I purchased an oversized book of maps for my car. I'll use my app to help me get there, but I'll use Rand McNally to urge me to Zoom Out! and pay attention to where I'm going.

Do You Bring Your Shoshin?

Shoshin is a concept in Zen Buddhism that means "beginner's mind."

Like children, beginners are open to new learning and discovering.

But as we collect experiences and knowledge in a subject, at a job, or in life, we tend to ignore new information.

Eventually we listen for information that confirms and validates what we already know and believe.

Unfortunately when we approach situations hauling our preconceptions, assumptions, and biases, our perspective becomes clouded, like smudged eyeglasses. We aren't open and eager, like beginners. We are dogmatic and opinionated, like experts.

Zen teacher Shunryu Suzuki remarked, "In the beginner's mind there are many possibilities, in the expert's mind there are few."

This impenetrable approach blocks our ability to learn anything new... unless we intentionally bring our Shoshin.

Marc Benioff, Founder and CEO of Salesforce, recently shared in *The New York Times*, "Having a beginner's mind informs my management style. I'm trying to listen deeply, and the beginner's mind is informing me to step back, so that I can create what wants to be not what was. I know that the future does not equal the past. I know I have to be here in the moment."

So how can we bring our Shoshin?
1. Lead with questions, not advice.
2. Respond, "Interesting. Tell me more."
3. Observe and listen.
4. Be curious... I wonder what makes her say that? I wonder what I'm missing.
5. Look for blindspots... we all have them.
6. Imagine the situation from the other person's perspective.
7. Stop being right.

In a world of bossy close-mindedness, we could use a bit more childlike openness.

Everyone Carries a Backstory... Our Journey is Who We Are

I walked into a workshop this week to find 6 people in the room:

1. A large Italian man who looks like a body-builder
2. A shy, tattooed man with a soft voice and wide eyes
3. A calm, completely bald man wearing a Hawaiian shirt
4. A stylish Asian-American woman with long, dark hair
5. A tall blond woman with a girlish voice and dramatic bangs
6. An African-American man wearing a flat-rimmed cap backwards

When the workshop started, the facilitator asked us to stand up and share, not what we do for a living, but a story about what led us to do what we do. Here's what I learned:

1. The large man is a chiropractor who takes steroids for an incurable disease.

2. The tattooed man is an ex-convict who saved himself through his health and is now a physical trainer for executives.

3. The bald man grew up in a Buddhist monastery and is now a sought-after business coach.

4. The Asian-American woman turned to nature to find sobriety and now runs a non-profit focused on the environment.

5. The blond grew up mute and dyslexic and is now a PhD in learning behaviors.

6. The African-American man grew up in the projects and is now a financially independent entrepreneur. (And he is engaged to the blond – they met on Tinder.)

Had we introduced ourselves with only our job titles, we would have been left with the stories we made up about each other, never discovering and connecting deeply.

We would have heard: I'm a chiropractor. I'm a personal trainer. I'm a coach. I'm a non-profit director. I'm a doctorate. I'm a businessman. It was an unexpected *Breakfast Club* experience.

What we do is not who we are. Our journey is who we are.

Titles shortchange us of discovering the journey – the why people have that title. Without the journey, we are left with our assumptions. And as a result, our connections remain shallow and lack trust.

So let's not stop at, "What do you do?"

Let's dig deeper and ask, "What led you to that job?" "What was your journey?" "What's your story?"

We Have Two Life Stories – Which One Runs Your Day?

We each have two life stories:

- the one behind us, and
- the one in front of us

The story behind us is our history, our experiences, our scars, our lessons learned.

The story in front of us is our future, our experiences to have, our scars to acquire, our lessons to learn.

The story behind us is rich with insights, perspective, and wisdom.
The story in front of us is ripe with opportunity, landscape, and wisdom to gain.

The story behind us is our comfort zone.
The story in front of us is our expandable, stretchable comfort zone.

The story behind us is our normal.
The story in front of us is our new normal.

We teach and mentor others based on the story behind us.
We seek teachers and mentors for the story in front of us.

The story behind us is a colorful painting we created.
The story in front of us is a blank canvas ready to be painted.

The story behind us is unchangeable.
The story in front of us is ours to unfold.

Every morning we wake to one story we can do nothing about.
Every morning we wake to another story we can do everything about.

Chapter 15

JOY & ENGAGEMENT

When Enterprise Asked Me, "Are You Somebody?"

I was traveling to keynote a leadership conference recently when I was upgraded to first class, offered a suite at the hotel, and treated to a celebratory dinner with my client.

But it was the experience at Enterprise that made me want to print "VIP" on my business cards.

When I arrived to pick up my rental car, I learned that my client had made arrangements for my car to be direct-billed, so I didn't even need to show a credit card. Direct-bill accounts must be unusual at this location, because Jessica, the rental agent, did a double-take at the computer. She looked at me a few times and then curiously said, "It looks like your car has been taken care of."

She paused and then eagerly inquired, "Are you somebody?"

I smiled amusingly, and proclaimed, "Yes, I am!"

My client went out of her way to help me feel important. Guess what I did. I delivered one of my best performances for her conference attendees.

Why? Because feeling important and significant fuels our confidence and self-esteem. And when our confidence spikes, we perform better and achieve more.

We operate at a higher level when we feel good about ourselves.

Every day we have the power and the privilege to manage (and interact with) others in a way that makes them feel ...like somebody! And when we do, we all win!

Should Joy be a Leader Competency?

What if joy was a leader's job? A skill required. An expectation of good leadership. A competency no less important than "Think strategically" or "Lead change."

Could we really be the source of joy? Well, if we have the power to influence misery and despair, then we certainly have the power to influence delight and happiness!

Wait! Aren't people supposed to be responsible for their own happiness? Why should this be our job as leaders? It's not our job; it our privilege. And it should become a priority. Because when we fuel happiness, delight, and respect, we get to work in it too – which is a lot more fun than working in animosity, indignation, and resentment

Still not convinced? Here are a few more reasons to embrace joy as a competency:

1. People watch you to determine how to act (called, "social cognitive theory")
2. Your joy will ripple (impacting your team/department/company)
3. Happy employees make happy customers (which generates more money)
4. High turnover and low engagement are costing you money and time (and frustration!)
5. You deserve to love your job too (in the end, it's all just a bullet on a resume)

So what do we need to do to create "joy as a leader's job"?

- Focus on making people successful
- Invite (and applaud) ideas and effort
- Admit mistakes and clear up miscommunications
- Replace "No!" as the first response with "Interesting. Say more."
- Get to know people personally
- Always assume people's good intent (instead of malice or idiocy)
- Treat people like new friends (instead of estranged family)
- Tell people how their work makes a difference
- Keep perspective (does that error really matter? what can we learn?)
- Laugh with people

What does all of this require? Courage, confidence, and relentless kindness. Daily. No exceptions.

Leaders Don't Laugh Much... But We Should

According to University of Maryland Professor Robert Povine's research on laughter, the higher up on a group's hierarchy, the less we laugh.

In other words, leaders don't laugh much. But we should and here's why...

Povine's research reveals that laughter is not about humor. It's about social bonding. We bond when we laugh together.

Studies show that when we bond, we strengthen the trust in our relationships. And nothing happens in leadership without trust.

So why don't bosses laugh more?

- Fear of perception (does being funny undermine my intelligence?)
- Too focused on the bottom line
- Other leaders aren't laughing (is it acceptable?)
- Sense of humor has atrophied (laughter is associated with play and adults don't play as much)
- Technology strangles laughter (more time on email and collaboration tools, means less time with people)

So how can we intentionally incorporate laughter into our leadership?

- Look for humorous situations and ironic moments
- Tell a go-to joke and ask others for their go-to jokes
- Share funny stories and invite others to do the same
- Self-deprecate (this underscore our humanity)
- Point out the insanity or inanity of situations
- Introduce improv games and team-building activities

Fortunately laughter is contagious... we actually smile and laugh at the sound of laughter (which explains the success of the Tickle Me Elmo doll!)

(As you exercise your funny bone, one enormous caution about inappropriate laughter. If you laugh at others (who are not laughing at themselves), mock certain groups, or giggle from nerves, you will contaminate trust.)

Laughter is an expression of joy. And when we intentionally make joy a part of our job as leaders, people look forward to working with us... no matter how grueling or stressful work may be.

---

3 Types of Happy Lives – Which One Will You Create Today?

According to psychologist Martin Seligman, founder of positive psychology (the study of happiness and emotional health), there are 3 types of happy lives:

1. Pleasant life
2. Engaged life
3. Meaningful life

Pleasant life: we gain happiness from pleasures, such as money, cars, toys, hobbies, adventures, and vacations

Engaged life: we gain happiness by creating social connections and fostering strong relationships

Meaningful life: we gain happiness by using our strengths and gifts to help others

Unfortunately, but not surprisingly, the easiest one – pursuing a pleasant life – has little bearing on our overall happiness and satisfaction.... that is, without pursuing an engaged life and a meaningful life.

Seligman found that the pursuit of pleasures only mattered when it was complemented by engagement and meaning.

Matthieu Ricard, a Tibetan Buddhist monk explains, "Thinking about yourself all the time and how to make things better for yourself is exhausting, stressful, and a quick route to unhappiness."

O.K. Conceptually, it's ideal to pursue a meaningful life, but how does all of this apply in the reality of our days? Through moments.

An engaged and meaningful life must first start with engaged and meaningful moments.

Lucky for us, opportunities to engage with others and create meaning (while pursuing pleasures) are plentiful!

Example:

- Pleasure Boss: "I need the team to sell more so I can get my bonus."

- Engaged Boss: "Employee, how are the kids and what are your career . . . . goals this year?"
- Meaningful Boss: "May I offer you some mentoring that might help you reach your goals?"

Example:

- Pleasure Passenger: "I love my first-class upgrade!"
- Engaged Passenger: "Hello, seat mate. Where are you headed today?"
- Meaningful Passenger: "Can I help you put that bag in the overhead?"

The secret ingredient: benevolence.

When we approach situations with compassion, generosity, kindness, friendship, and humanity, it's impossible not to boost our own happiness and satisfaction ...even while enjoying the pleasures of life.

Ignore Engagement. Obsess Over Involvement.

Employee engagement is like the war on terror. We're not sure exactly what it means; we can't exactly describe it; we don't know what to do about it; we never really know if we are making any progress; and we will never know if we have won.

According to the Gallop Organization, only 29% of employees are engaged and 71% are disengaged. As defined by Gallop, employees are engaged when they "work with passion and feel connected to the company."

These stats and this definition confound me. As a leader, I'm already feeling responsible for the success of people above me, below me, and beside me. Now I'm supposed to be responsible for their passion and connection to the company? In the words of the investors on the reality show *Shark Tank*, "I'm out."

Every day, my focus is to lead better, execute effectively, innovate constantly, and make a difference.

So I choose to ignore "employee engagement" and instead I obsess over "employee involvement." And then engagement takes care of itself.

When employees are involved, they are included in decisions, they participate in improving processes, they undertake planning and strategy, and they are immersed in execution. As a result, they are committed, engrossed, and concerned.

As a leader of my own team, I don't have a clue whether my people are engaged – and frankly I don't give a damn.

What I do care about is that they are involved – constantly. And as a result:
- my people are committed to the company's success and the success of our clients
- they are included in decisions
- they participate in improving processes
- they are engrossed in projects and program launches
- they are relentlessly responding to each other and to clients

Here's the difference:
- With engagement, people are passionate and connected to the company.

- With involvement, people are committed to, engrossed in, and concerned about the success of the company and its clients.
- With engagement, managers are responsible for an employee's feelings of passion and connection. (This is distracting and can ultimately breed entitlement and disrespect.)
- With involvement, managers are responsible for involving employees. And employees are responsible for their own feelings.

Our job as leaders is to involve people. Their job is to stay involved. After that they can assess their own passion and connection.

Chapter 16

RECOGNITION & CELEBRATION

Lead with Woo-Hoos not Tsk-Tsks!

Our people crave woo-hoos, high-fives, fist bumps, and applause.

Instead we question them in meetings, overrule them in emails, and judge them in performance reviews.

Which is all rather unnecessary because they are already questioning their self-worth and judging their performance on a daily basis.

Is flaming their self-doubt really the best use of our role as their leader?

What they really need from us is a spotlight on their wins, a highlighter for their progress, and limelight for their successes. Our people need us to celebrate them!

What does celebration look like?

- a shout-out: "You're a rockstar! "Great idea!" "Congratulations!"
- a compliment: "Your report was solid."
- a progress marker: "I'm so impressed with how you are managing this project."
- an effort acknowledgement: "I love that you took a chance to improve it."
- a good news advancement: "The client loves it. Great work!"

And the reality is that it's a heckuva lot more fun to lead people in celebration than it is to lead them in condemnation.

I Carried a Buffalo Trophy Through the Airport.

I had the privilege and pleasure of speaking in Buffalo, NY for the Project Management Institute (PMI) annual conference.

At the end of my keynote, the conference organizers surprised me with a trophy.

And not just any trophy... a solid, wooden block engraved with my name, topped with a large, brass buffalo, standing 13 inches tall and weighing 3 pounds. It is not insignificant.

I gushed in delight. And then I wondered... how was I going to transport it in my small carry-on luggage?

Determined to take it home, I opted to carry the Buffalo Trophy through the airport, like an Emmy.

And as a result, I made a lot of friends:

- The TSA security agent and I laughed about bringing bigger luggage next time.
- The waitress and other patrons at the airport restaurant congratulated me, wanting to know more about my award.
- Passengers in the boarding area enjoyed the ongoing banter sparked by the buffalo.
- Two guys on the airtrain loved it so much they insisted on taking a selfie with me and the buffalo.

Here's what I discovered from carrying the Buffalo Trophy:

1. Significant and Personal Recognition is Powerful
The trophy is an indisputable statement of PMI's appreciation. And it was unnecessary... I received a nice fee for my keynote. But PMI went out of their way to ensure that I felt recognized, appreciated, and special all the way home.

2. People are Eager to Connect but Need a Reason
The Buffalo Trophy is noticeable and peculiar - an instant conversation piece, making it easy to connect and engage with complete strangers. I had so much fun carrying the Buffalo Trophy that I am might take it with me on my next trip.

And rest assured, when PMI-Buffalo calls me again, I'll make time for them!

IN A FLASH!

To Stop Good Behavior, Ignore It

Police officers are charged with catching people doing something wrong. Ward Clapham, a retired veteran of the Royal Canadian Mounted Police, described it as "always looking for the dark side."

In 2002 Ward decided to shift the obedience-by-fear paradigm. He started catching kids doing something right, polite, safe, or kind.

He issued Positive Tickets to kids he saw crossing the road safely, picking up litter, wearing a bike helmet, or doing their homework.

And to add significance, he allowed kids to exchange their tickets for pizza, gift certificates, or movie passes. To his surprise, some kids held on to their tickets to display at home, like a trophy for being a good person.

But it's not about the tickets! It's about the relationship he built with young people in his community. By recognizing their good behavior and acknowledging their worth, he gained their trust.

People at work also crave "Positive Tickets." According to research, more than 50% of employees say they would look for another job if their manager did not appreciate or acknowledge their work.

As leaders, we should be issuing Positive Tickets every day! People who feel recognized have higher self-esteem which leads to greater contributions. We all work harder when we feel good about ourselves.

Positive Tickets can be as simple as a thank you email or card. Remember, it's not about the ticket; it's about the relationship and the trust that recognition engenders – essential for our success in leading!

Apparently, puppies crave Positive Tickets too. The motto posted in the puppy training room at my pet store is: "If you want to stop good behavior, ignore it."

My Favorite Part of Football is the End

My favorite part of the football game is the moment the clock runs out and the opposing teams converge on the field. I enjoy watching the players and coaches shake hands, give bear hugs, and reconnect like comrades.

In spite of the competition, they connect to:
- show respect and understanding
- congratulate on a game well-played
- acknowledge and appreciate their shared experience

So why don't we get more of this humanity off the football field?

We could blame technology...

Studies show that the less we need each other, the less we pay attention to, interact with, and care about others. The independence we get from technology actually disconnects us from others and numbs are compassion.

Remember life before the GPS... we actually had to ask people for directions, and they actually stopped what they were doing to help us. Today, we just plug in an address and drive. More efficient, but less connected.

And the less connection we have, the less compassion we feel.

So what can we do to reignite connection and fuel compassion?
- Play! (engage in sports and games)
- Talk to people (instead of typing on the phone)
- Assume everyone has a story to share
- Appreciate their story by asking about their experience
- Volunteer (see how others live!)

Football is all about connection. Players engage with and rely on each other – so they are constantly fueling their compassion. The rest of us... we must be more intentional about generating connection or we risk going numb.

Shift Thanksgiving to Celebrate-giving

Thanksgiving is traditionally the time of year to give thanks and be grateful.

But when we already say "thank you" customarily to everyone we work or interact with, how can we create a different impact?

Celebrate people!

When we celebrate people, we publicly praise their contributions, validate their growth and development, and bear witness to their importance as human beings.

So what's the impact? Remarkable.

Celebration is powerful brain food that releases endorphins and serotonins, which:

- creates feelings of safety and confidence
- enables people to learn and grow
- transforms skeptics into supporters and stress into success

To celebrate people meaningfully, there are 3 essentials:

1. Specificity: people are eager to know how they can get more praise
2. Authenticity: if we deliver praise sincerely, they will listen to and trust us
3. Intentionality: it has to be on purpose, not as an afterthought

What do Celebration Words sound like?

- Your service to the client is above-and-beyond!
- You are a joy to work with!
- Your mentoring has helped me think strategically.
- Your friendship makes me a kinder person.
- This is delicious! You are an amazing cook!

Celebrating others has the power to influence, ignite, and inspire any relationship at work or in life. Almost makes the ordinary "thanks" look like a consolation prize....

Add Some Gusto to that Gratitude!

Woo-hoo! The annual holiday to be more grateful has arrived! And every year, experts apprise us of all the benefits we could reap personally by being more grateful: lower blood pressure, less stress, better sleep, stronger mental clarity, happiness...

But what about the influence that being grateful can have on others?

There are two behavioral theories that get triggered when we acknowledge and appreciate others:

1. Self-Delusion Bias
2. Spotlight Effect

Self-Delusion Bias
People who feel good about themselves tend to perform better.

When we express gratitude by acknowledging someone, we fuel their self-esteem and boost their confidence. And with boosted confidence, people exert even more effort in hopes of obtaining more self-esteem fuel.

Spotlight Effect
People who feel their actions are noticed ("spotlighted") by someone tend to operate more effectively just to impress the person watching.

When we express gratitude by appreciating someone's actions, we spotlight that action. Just by noticing, we spark that person's desire to perform that action even better in hopes that we continue to notice and spotlight that action again.

The secret, however, is in the specificity. Running around yelling "Thanks, Bob!" "Thanks, Mary!" is ineffective because it feels contrived and insincere.

For specificity, we need to put some gusto in our gratitude!

- Thank you for the way you always make us healthy dinners.
- I appreciate the difference you make on the team with your solutions.
- I am grateful for your perseverance in getting us the right answer.
- I am in awe of your constant kindness toward strangers.

If we want our gratitude to be significant and ripple with impact beyond the holidays, we need to add a little gusto to our gratitude!

Chapter 17

LEADING

Are You Trying to Prove Your Success?

Last week I listened with pride as Ian authentically shared some revelations about his own leadership title. He was delivering his final presentation to 60 of his colleagues (Vice Presidents, Directors, Managers, and Supervisors) in our Leadership Mentoring Program.

I recorded his presentation. These are his exact words:

- I had just been promoted to my role as a supervisor. As I entered this program, I thought, "I'm going to prove myself as a leader. I'm going to get all my work done. I'm going to shine. I'm going to prove to my superiors that I can do a good job."
- But during this program, I realized that my superiors put me in that position because they knew I already had those skills.
- Where I can flourish is investing time in those around me.
- Being able to improve their work ethic, help them with their difficulties, and highlight their successes has been how I have grown as a leader.
- Making the people around me better has made me a better person in general.
- I've done that by becoming less of a need-filler and more of a want-creator with those around me.

Bravo!

Here's what we can glean from Ian's insights:

1. Stop trying to prove that you are successful
   (they already know it or they would not have given you the job!)
2. Start investing in the success of your people
   (that will make you a better person)
3. Shift your focus from filling people's needs to creating their desire for success *(less need-filling, more want-creating)*
4. Genuinely share your experience in striving to become a better leader and a better person *(vulnerability will differentiate you and influence others)*
5. Never confuse your title with your contribution *(a leadership title does not make one a leader; only actions in service of others' success do)*

Being a leader is actually not about you at all. Our ability to authentically admit and act on that will catapult the difference we make in the service of others.

Do You Lead with Ubuntu?

Ubuntu (oo-boon-too): an old African word meaning "humanity," beautifully translated as, "I am because we are."

Essentially, we can only experience our humanity through our interactions with others. Ubuntu compels us to look after each other with kindness, compassion, and generosity of spirit.

I discovered Ubuntu staying at a Radisson. It was 3:00am when I called the front desk looking for some medicine for a deep cut on my ankle that I had ignored all day. The throbbing became unbearable.

Sheila answered the phone, but couldn't even locate a Band-Aid. Distressingly I winched, "Then I'll need to find a 24-hour pharmacy..."

Quickly discerning my pain, Sheila announced, "Wait! Let me see what I can do." She then enlisted a colleague to cover the front desk while she ran across the street to another hotel to find some medicine for me.

Sheila met me in the lobby with pain-relieving ointment, bandages, and a lot of sympathy.

In our short interaction, Sheila alleviated my pain, saved my meeting the next day, and inspired me with her patience, resourcefulness, and benevolence. That's the power of Ubuntu! Like Sheila, in any moment, we can lead with Ubuntu.

Once we realize that we are who we are *because of* (not in spite of) the people we work with, we can intentionally embrace opportunities to make a difference.

How?

- Listening to and learning about others
- Mentoring, coaching, sponsoring others as they pursue goals
- Recognizing, appreciating others and celebrating their wins
- Being patient in the midst of pressure
- Seeking first to understand in the face of judgment
- Going out of our way to help and contribute

We don't get paid for bringing Ubuntu to our jobs. But leading with Ubuntu, we have the power to be not only better leaders, but better human beings.

Beware of the Lulu Delusion

My niece Lulu is six. Her 1st grade teacher announced, "Lulu, I'm looking for a leader in class. Can you be a leader?"

Lulu came home and frustratingly announced, "She said she wants me to be a leader, but she does all the talking! How am I supposed to lead if she never stops talking?"

We all risk a similar Lulu Delusion – we think leading is about talking.

But we lead best when we aren't just talking. We lead best when we:

- Listen and empathize
- Inquire, discover, and learn
- Mentor and role-model
- Recognize, appreciate, and applaud
- Own mistakes and apologize
- Help others be successful

Lulu is right. People talk too much.

But what Lulu doesn't yet understand is that being asked to be "the leader" is just the beginning of the leadership journey, not the end.

Manage with Fear; Lead with Love

Manage with Fear.

We manage things (not people). We manage time, budgets, calendars, resources.

What should we fear? That we won't have enough time, we won't have enough money, and we won't have enough resources. We should fear that things won't go right. We should fear that something will go wrong.

Fear is good. It keeps us vigilant, conscientious, intentional, observant, attentive, and meticulous. Without fear, we risk errors, mistakes, failures, omissions, complacency, even apathy.

Lead with Love.

We lead people (not things). We lead our employees, our peers, our supervisors, our customers, our children.

What should we love? We should love contributing to their success. We should love mentoring them. We should love watching them grow, develop, and thrive. We should love helping others become bigger, better, bolder versions of themselves.

Love is good. It keeps leading about other people and not about us. It keeps work in perspective. We own our communication. We hold others and ourselves accountable. We operate with a conviction of their potential to succeed on our team or elsewhere.

Leading without Love.

Without love, we risk narcissism, arrogance, self-importance, and audacity. And we usually end up leading with frustration, annoyance, exasperation, judgment, dislike, disdain, distrust, disgust, anger, or hate.

When we don't lead with love we are angry and irritable, we are impatient and we lack compassion, we are incensed at everyone's incompetence, we believe people are purposefully sabotaging our success, and we are disgusted by the politics and policies.

Leading with love requires vulnerability. It's about constantly becoming a better leader. It's about a commitment to others becoming bigger, better, bolder, smarter versions of themselves as a result of engaging with us.

What Does Kindness Have To Do With Leading?

Without kindness work sucks – for us and for the people who work with us.

As leaders, our success lies in our ability to keep good people involved, committed, contributing, growing themselves, and developing others.

But good people don't trust unkind leaders – no one likes following a jerk.

The good news is that being kind is the one thing we have 100% control of every day in every moment. We cannot control customers, co-workers, personalities, the markets, the weather, the traffic, or other jerks.

We can only control how we treat each other – our responses, our character, and our commitment to serve others' success.

We can be kind without exception for stress, pressure, job titles, job levels, or our own momentary lack of self-confidence.

Next time we lose patience, yell, belittle, or disparage another, let's let a breath in and ask ourselves, am I being kind or am I being kind of a jerk?

And then own the responsibility we have at every moment and with everyone to be human first.

You Don't Need New Toys

Problems are like new toys – they need figuring out.

People bring us their problems like they're bringing us a Rubik's cube, a Lego set, or a new video game – insisting that we play too.

Why do they bring us their new toys?

Because they know we can figure them out. We always have solutions, ideas, or key information.

So they drop their toys on our desk, eager to let us play.

And they're right! We can figure them out and quite often we love to. But we already have enough toys to play with.

When people bring us new toys, there are 5 things we can offer to help them move forward:

1. Perspective
2. Information
3. Resources
4. Mentoring
5. Encouragement

Before anyone starts sharing their new toys, ask them first which of these they need from you.

Then make them take their toys with them when they leave.

Our job is not to collect the most toys but to help our people learn how to play better with their own.

Read Fiction. Lead Better.

I just returned from a family vacation, and, I have a confession: I read a fiction book.

Typically I justify time away from work by poring over leadership tomes. So I inhaled this fiction book like a sinful treat.

And then I discovered that my guilty pleasure actually helps me lead better.

According to recent research, even short bouts of reading fiction:

- improves our understanding of other human beings
- helps us see the world from others' points of view
- reminds us that people hold varying perspectives and beliefs

The act of reading fiction allows us to engage in what researchers call "Experience Thinking" – our emotional connection to the characters causes us to explain and empathize with their behaviors, even if we don't agree with them.

How does this help us in the non-fiction world? By increasing our social cognition and strengthening our emotional perception, we become better at collaborating, empathizing, and connecting with others.

Essentially reading a fiction book is training for our human interactions, no different than lifting weights is training for our muscles.

Just by reading fiction, we can transform our impact as leaders and as human beings (and enjoy our downtime more).

Is Your Backstage Showing?

When I go to see a play, I want to be entertained by what's on the stage. I don't want to know what's happening behind the curtains with the actors, the directors, or the stage crew.

Activity on the backstage just distracts my experience in the audience.

Similarly, we shouldn't give our employees a backstage pass either.

What's on our backstage?

- our stress
- our overbooked calendar
- our fight with our boss
- our disapproval of an executive decision
- our bad mood, distress, or anxiety
- our personal career angst

Venting, complaining, gossiping, and even showing up late and frazzled are just various ways of revealing our backstage.

And all of that swirling chaos is about us. It's not about them. They don't need it, and frankly they don't want it.

The backstage taints their experience of us as their intrepid leader, distracts their focus from goals on the front stage, and does not contribute to their progress.

The next time you are about to pull back the curtains and share, vent, gripe, or gossip, consider whether it is in the best service of the other person's success and of yours as a leader.

Then keep the backstage on the backstage.

Our front stage is our commitment to serve people's success; divulging our backstage betrays that commitment.

Are You Gratified When People Bring You Problems?

Colin Powell (retired four-star general in the US Army) once said, "The day the soldiers stop bringing you their problems is the day you stopped leading them. They have either lost confidence that you can help them or concluded that you do not care. Either case is a failure of leadership."

Like you, I run a team. I get it. We're busy. And sometimes we wish people would just figure out their own jobs, and stop dumping problems at our feet. We have enough of our own!

And then Colin Powell's admonition gives us pause. Imagine the silence we would experience if our people stopped reaching out for our guidance and partnership. If our phone goes silent, we have failed.

But this doesn't mean that we are required to rescue people.
- We don't need to think for them.
- We don't need to fix each crisis.
- We don't have to give them all the answers.
- We don't even have to tolerate repeated questions.

But we better hope they keep seeking our assistance.

And here's how we can encourage our people to do just that:
- regard each problem as an opportunity to develop people
- implore people to bring us new and different problems
- demand that people identify two solutions for every problem they unload
- coach, mentor, and train people so they learn and grow into bigger problems
- urge people to capture their learnings in job aides and quick guides

Regardless of how busy and stressed we are, we want our "soldiers" to call on us. We want them to have confidence in us as their intrepid leader. We want them to know that we always care about their success.

That's how we earn the title "boss" day after day.

The Secret to Good Drivers and Bosses...Predictability

While on vacation with my family, a van crossed directly in my path like a deer. I didn't see it ...until I crashed into it. The airbags went off, our car was destroyed. It was completely unpredictable. (Fortunately, no one was hurt.)

It's predictability that allows thousands of drivers to safely traverse freeways at 70mph during rush hour. We can predict what other drivers are going to do because of their break lights, their turn signal indicators, and even their horns.

But when a car races by like Mario Andretti, dodging between vehicles without any indication, we are all forced to deal with the driver's unpredictability. This causes fear, anger, and sometimes accidents.

Similarly, it's our unpredictability as a boss that causes the most challenges for our teams. When people can predict how we will operate, they can better engage with and support us. But when we change lanes without warning, our unpredictability causes frustration, aggravation, and often conflict. And this fractures the foundation of trust we need to lead.

What makes us unpredictable? Our:

- foggy communications
- unclear expectations
- failure to respond or share information
- emotional outbursts
- unexplained changes
- lack of follow-up and accountability

As an example, when we change directions without any conversation or get mad at someone without any explanation, we are like a bad driver changing lanes without signaling.

By becoming more predictable through our communications, we can not only foster more effective relationships, we can actually develop people in the process. How? Sharing our approach to various situations and decisions actually allows others to learn and improve.

Ultimately, when we are predictable in relationships, we can best respond, support, and serve each other's success. Predictability makes driving cars, teams, and families actually work ...without accidents.

IN A FLASH!

Do You Deal in Hope?

Napoleon Bonaparte said, "A leader is a dealer in hope."

That describes every start-up CEO I represented as a corporate attorney in Silicon Valley. Each one was hard-working and demanding. Yet each one intentionally painted a picture of the future to inspire people to join the company and contribute to its success.

Research conducted by Gallup Organization asked 10,000 individuals what they want from their boss, and they discovered four overarching desires:

- Compassion: care personally and individually
- Stability: job constancy
- Trust: behavioral predictability
- Hope: inspiration for a better future

Hope is the conviction that our work today actually matters, and that tomorrow will be even better as a result.

So how can we practically "deal in hope" on a regular basis?

- Shout a battle cry (a vision, a purpose)
- Choose positive, encouraging language ("That was a great insight!")
- Connect activity with impact ("Your work makes a difference because...")
- Employ inspirational posters, emails, and tag lines ("Success is on the other side of fear")
- Be a role model (people mold their own behavior by watching what we do)
- Recognize effort ("I appreciate your attempt at helping the client.")
- Celebrate small victories ("We're getting closer! Woo-hooo!")
- Express belief in others ("You can do this!")

The opposite of dealing in hope is trafficking in fear. And fear shuts down motivation, enthusiasm, collaboration, and innovation. Just ask anyone who hates their boss. They don't feel hope. They feel fear... fear of being judged, criticized, blamed, and even fired.

Jeff, a manager in one of my Managing and Leading programs, shared how he regularly deals in hope. He doesn't just delegate an assignment or project; he makes an invitation to his people with a simple yet powerful phrase delivered enthusiastically, yet sincerely:

> *"This is your chance for greatness."*

I Measure My Leadership from a Bicycle

Since 2011, I've biked across the country, up the East coast, down the West coast, across Iowa, and from Crater Lake to Yosemite.

With my 6th ride, I pedaled from Banff National Park in Canada to Yellowstone National Park in Wyoming. 813 miles.

Why all the cycling adventures? Because I love that with my own muscles, I've scaled mountains, seen national parks, met interesting people, and discovered corners of the country I would have otherwise missed in a car.

As I pedaled across the border, I reflected on each ride from a personal and professional standpoint.

And then it struck me... I can measure my growth as a leader from my bicycle.

When I did my first bicycle adventure, I never really left work. Thanks to my cell phone and my computer, I managed to cycle and kiss worms in the day-to-day weeds throughout the entire ride. My team still laughs remembering how I pedaled over the Continental Divide while conducting a conference call!

But this time was different. I didn't bring my laptop. I wasn't on any conference calls. I wasn't leading any webinars. I only brought my iPad and a book to read.

So what changed over those 7 years? My leadership skills:

- I improved my delegation abilities and learned how to trust
- I partnered with my team to hire and expand the team
- I learned how to develop and empower others
- I improved my communication skills

While I was in contact with my team, I was confident they could lead without me, because I prepared them to lead.

I'm always working on being a better boss. Now I test my improved leadership skills from my bicycle.

How do you measure your growth as a leader?

Chapter 18

TRUST

Accelerating Trust

If you want to influence anyone, trust is imperative. People only follow people they trust, regardless of titles.

When you have the privilege of leading or mentoring others, trust is your bedrock to success.

If you attempt to lead or mentor without it, you breed micromanagement, resentment, disinvolvement, and even active disruption.

Here are 7 ways to accelerate and strengthen the trust you need in order to lead others:

1. Commonalities

When we discover something in common, we feel connected. Commonalities bond people automatically. As an exmple, I love dogs. So I am instantly more trusting of others who love dogs. Seek out common grounds.

2. Interest

When we sincerely seek to learn about someone else, to appreciate our diversity, to understand their choices, experiences, and situations, we fuel trust. When we lack interest, however, we feed assumptions, judgments, and even prejudices – theirs and ours. Express a sincere interest in your differences.

3. Compassion

When we offer empathy rather than indifference, we kindle trust. Before thrusting a change onto people, we need to first meet them where they are. Be empathic and understanding.

4. Experiences

When we have experiences with others – projects, workshops, off-sites, retreats, community volunteering – we strengthen trust. There is a reason we still have that friend from high school. Our lives may be completely different now, but the experiences we shared as teenagers bonded us. Intentionally create experiences to bring you together.

5. Vulnerability

When we share something personal or reveal some fears or aspirations, our vulnerability invites theirs, which promotes trust. We trust people who are genuine and we disconnect from people who are inauthentic. Drop your defenses and expose your authenticity.

6. Integrit

When we do the right thing even when no one is looking, when we share credit for an idea or the success of a project, and when we follow up as we promised, we operate with integrity. And people trust people with integrity. Our lies, however – even little white lies – will invalidate that trust. Demonstrate honesty of character.

7. Consistency

When we execute, when we communicate, when we show up, time and time again, people trust us. Our consistency accelerates trust. Exhibit consistent actions.

If you want to uplevel your influence, start with trust. Because if trust was so easy to generate, it wouldn't be so valuable.

It's Hard to Distrust Up Close

Upon reviewing the National Geographic documentary entitled, *Gender Revolution*, Dr. Oz declared, "It's hard to hate up close."

Such a powerful statement. Just think of the prolific hatred online – people hating complete strangers while hiding behind keyboards...

What does this have to do with our commitment to lead while managing? Everything. It's not just hard to hate up close; it's hard to distrust up close. So our job is to get up close.

As managers who lead, we are in a constant battle with distrust – it rages like wildfire. And when distrust looms, it's nearly impossible for us to make a difference with people.

So how does "up close" alter distrust?

Disconnection breeds distrust. The more disconnected people are from each other, the more they assume, speculate, and postulate. Essentially we make up stories. And unchecked, stories yield suspicion and distrust.

But when we are "up close" with people, we get to know them and they get to know us. We discover their experiences, we invalidate our assumptions. And from this personal connection, trust flourishes.

So how do we get up close with people?
- Be curious about others
- Ask about their experiences – personally and professionally
- Stop relying on email and texts to connect and communicate
- Pick up the phone
- Use video conferencing (this is a game-changer for my team)
- Show up in person – be with people
- Seek their side of the story
- Address conflict intentionally
- Create together: plans, ideas, solutions

As we connect with people personally, our assumptions, fabrications, and speculations about them – and theirs about us – evaporate. And that allows trust to prosper. We just need to get up close.

The Magic of Mirroring

As humans, we are drawn to people when we find something in common. As an example, I am crazy about my dogs, and I instantly like people who share a similar dog obsession.

This commonality leads to rapport, positive feelings, and even increased trust.

But what if we don't have anything in common with another person? We can create it through Behavior-Mirroring.

Behavior-Mirroring occurs when we match a person's posture, gestures, facial expressions, speech pattern, attitude, or verbalization.

Matching verbalization is the easiest mirror to use. Just repeat what the other person has said. "So you're saying you want to move the meeting to Thursday?"

Not only does Behavior-Mirroring create the requisite commonality to fuel rapport and trust, it forces us to slow down and process the information. And most importantly, it actively assures the other person that we are truly listening.

Want to see it in action? Observe a savvy waiter repeat your order back to you word for word. And then notice how your confidence in that waiter escalates.

Because trust makes or breaks our success as managers (and mentors), we need to intentionally engage the magic of mirroring to generate commonality, rapport, and connection.

Assumption-Crushing Questions

Questions are the gateway to relationships.

But questions require a pause. And in our 140-character tweeting, 10-second snapping, emoji-dominated world, we don't often pause.

Instead we defer to our propensity to swagger and solve. We either entertain people with our "extremely interesting" Facebook-post-able story, or we bombard with some unsolicited advice and recommendations... while people pine for our curiosity, sincerity, and interest.

Questions fuel trust and strengthen relationships by suspending our swagger and crushing the assumptions we make about people, their situations, and their experiences. By intentionally asking questions, we force ourselves to learn more before offering advice and ideas.

In doing so, we demonstrate our commitment to connect.

5 Assumption-Crushing, Trust-Building Questions:
1. What was that experience like? (a great follow-up question to "how was your weekend / meeting / vacation / event?")
2. What do you want to be, do, or accomplish (today, next week, month, year)?
3. How did you reach that decision?
4. What are you already doing that's helping you get there?
5. Where do you need the most help? How can I help?

People are starved for the connections that are created through sincere inquiry. By simply asking a few assumption-crushing questions, we can create and invest in relationships that matter.

Are you a Sentence Stepper?

Stepping on someone's sentence isn't a big deal, is it? I do it all the time.

I excitedly respond to what someone is saying... even before they finish their sentence. Or I have a perfect story that relates to their story or something funny to share that adds to theirs. But if I wait until they're done talking, I might forget.

Clearly it's just my enthusiasm and passion (sometimes my impatience and irritation); so what's the problem with a little sentence-stepping?

It's rude and disrespectful. And it contaminates trust.
- When we intentionally listen to someone, they trust us a little more.
- When we step on someone's sentences, they trust us a little less.

As leaders, trust is everything – people only follow people they trust. So trust must be our constant commitment, not a checkbox on a to-do list.

The trust people have in us is strengthened or splintered in each interaction.

Sentence-stepping doesn't strengthen trust; it splinters it. Instead of demonstrating our passion and enthusiasm, it actually demonstrates our selfishness and disrespect.

When every conversation either contributes to or contaminates trust, we need to step on our tongue instead of their sentence.

Chapter 19

INFLUENCE

People Support That Which They Help Create

People support that which they help create.

In behavioral economics, this is called "Participatory Bias" – people are more inclined to support decisions they help to make and solutions they help to create, even if the end result is not theirs.

Having participated, people are more willing to defend the outcome. The ego won't allow them to support the process and oppose it at the same time.

The opposite is also true. When we don't include people in decisions, projects, or solutions, they are more likely to resist, oppose, and even sabotage the end result. Knowing this, why wouldn't we go out of our way to create opportunities for people to participate, even when we don't need them to?

We cannot ignore the enormous influence participation has on human behavior. The simple act of including someone:

- helps that person feel valued, recognized, and appreciated
- increases their engagement and patronage
- fosters their effectiveness through understanding, learning, and discovery
- encourages their creativity and innovation

Easy ways to create participation:

- Solicit suggestions for improving the team, the meeting, a project, or a process
- Ask someone new every week for their perspective on an issue
- Seek advice on solving a problem from someone not involved with it
- Request the team's help in generating new ideas or approaches
- Nominate people for a task force, a committee, or a development program

If we want to be great leaders, we need to intentionally provide people with the opportunity to participate, contribute, and make a difference.

Change the Frame. Change the Game.

People makes choices based on frames – the way a problem or situation is presented. Technically dubbed the "Framing Effect," it wields incredible power on the mindset.

People will act differently even when presented with the same situation just framed differently. People choose 80% lean meat but avoid 20% fat meat. People willingly accept a process or procedure with 75% success rate but hesitate on one that has a 25% failure rate.

As leaders, the frames we use dictate the actions our people take. We can influence people's choices merely by the way we frame a situation. How do we create those frames? With our words, our tone, and our body language.

As an example, I called the dog groomer to schedule an appointment. The woman who answered groaned, "uh-oh! Bad news! We don't have any availability for 6 weeks." I was instantly in a bad mood and walked away without making an appointment.

I then phoned another groomer. She said "Good news! We have an opening as early as June 12!" (which, by the way, was also 6 weeks away) I was instantly in a good mood and booked the appointment immediately.

Framing is pervasive. Every day frames are affecting how we experience the day. We just aren't paying attention. And that's a missed opportunity.

- Is it partly cloudy or mostly sunny?
- Are you fixing people's weaknesses or leveraging their strengths?
- Do you have problems or opportunities?
- Are you lost or on an adventure?
- Do you scoff at global warming but tremble at climate change?
- Is there a 25% chance of failure or a 75% chance of success?
- Does your team make mistakes or are they learning lessons?
- Are you faced with issues or challenges?

Green Bay Packers Coach Mike McCarthy fitted his team for Super Bowl rings the day before Super Bowl XLV. Why? He wanted them to walk into the game with a Super Bowl champion mindset. So he used the fitting to intentionally frame the situation for his players. Their actions followed and they won the game. Afterwards, Linebacker A.J. Hawk said of the coach's brazen move, "It made things real for us."

Why should you care about frames? Because the words you use every day are creating the frames that influence your people's mindset. And your people are making decisions and taking actions based on that mindset.

Your words are powerful. Choose them intentionally.

The Power of the Label

My teacher in 2nd grade wrote the word "enthusiastic" on my report card. My parents beamed with pride. So I continued to be enthusiastic. Teachers continued to write the word on my report card. And my parents continued to beam.

Labels are a powerful influence.

Diagnosis Bias

When a person gets labeled by someone they admire, respect, or value, they mold and shape their behaviors to fit that label. This phenomenon is called "diagnosis bias."

Ultimately, once someone is diagnosed, their brain looks for evidence to confirm that diagnosis.

The label is so powerful that it literally causes that person to start acting out that label through their behavior and decisions. And once they start acting out a label, they perpetuate it as they continue to reinforce and reaffirm it with more behaviors and decisions. Essentially people confirm the diagnosis they are given through their own actions.

Parents Label Children:

A mom says, "Sally is shy." The more Sally hears that she is shy, the more she acts shy, which then confirms that Sally is, in fact, shy.

Bosses Label Employees:

Jane has been identified as an "up-and-coming leader at the company." Bob, however, has been told he might not be cut out for sales.

- The more Jane hears her label, the more Jane acts like an up-and-coming leader, which confirms for her and everyone else that Jane is, in fact, an up-and-coming leader.
- Bob's diagnosis shapes his behavior, and his sales slip, which then confirms the diagnosis that he is, in fact, not cut out for sales.

Brand Your Labels Carefully

When someone respects and admires us, we must apply labels carefully. When we brand that person with a label (ex: smart, dumb, strategic, ineffective, leader, follower), they will embrace the behaviors of that label and then mirror the expectations we have for them. Invariably, they adopt the characteristics of that label.

How can we use labels more vigilantly?

- Notice the labels you use for people – consider that your label may be perpetuating their behavior
- Select labels for people based on the behavior you want, not the behavior you see currently
- Employ empowering titles and nicknames for people (ex: Queen of People Success, King of Sales, Client Engagement Specialist, Product Guru, Leader of Leaders)

Pay attention to the labels you use and wield this superpower with diligence and intentionality.

We Get To Control the Environment

We cannot control people's skills and abilities. We cannot control their attitude or motivation. We can influence these, but we do not get to control them.

And believing that we can is one of our biggest challenges as leaders.

The only thing we can control as leaders is the environment and context.

- We can ensure they have a safe, clean, well-lit place to work.
- We can provide them with the resources and information they need to be successful.
- We can make sure they have clear expectations and fog-free communications from us.
- We can challenge them to grow, offering our steadfast support in the process.
- We can even free them from bullies, jerks, and other saboteurs.

But we do a disservice to them and to ourselves as leaders when we pretend that we can control their skills, abilities, attitudes, or motivation.

Our job is to influence these, and we do that through the environment we create and the context we supply.

We can provide them training to acquire a new skill and we can even dangle a bonus in hopes of cajoling them into learning and applying that new skill. But in the end, only they control what they will learn from and do with that training, and if they'll do it with a smile or a scowl.

By staying focused on the environment we can control, we shift to our people personal responsibility for what they can control – their own success.

Self-Delusion vs. Self-Deflation

We all believe the world revolves around us. It's self-delusional. As leaders, we need to fuel this self-delusion in others. Studies show that when people feel valued and important, they feel good about themselves because they matter. Their self-esteem spikes and they achieve more.

To fuel self-delusion:

- Put people in charge of something
- Remember names, birthdays, events
- Comment on the impact of people's efforts
- Solicit their ideas, opinions, perspective
- Include people in decisions

Unfortunately, some leaders spend an inordinate amount of time demonstrating that in fact the world does not revolve around these other people. While it's usually unconscious or unintentional, the impact is nonetheless the same.

To ensure people know the world does not revolve around them:

- Implement lots of rules, policies, and procedures so people don't go rogue
- Micro-manage constantly by focusing on how people do their job so they know they cannot be trusted on their own
- Consistently cancel meetings with people so they know how busy and important you are
- Answer phone calls, emails, and texts in the middle of your conversation with them so they know that someone or something trumps whatever it was they were prattling on about
- Keep it a big secret that their work makes a difference
- Talk incessantly about the amazing things you do at work and at home without showing any curiosity or interest in them
- Make lots of decisions without their input

When we burst self-delusion, we get self-deflation. People's self-esteem collapses with the reality that they aren't that valued and important; that they really don't matter. And with low self-esteem, people achieve less, sometimes even sabotaging their own success.

While it might make you feel more important and valuable when you feed your self-delusion, know that you do so at the expense of theirs. When you want to make a shift in your leadership impact, it doesn't get any easier than letting others be the center of their universe.

When the Self-Serving Bias Does Not Serve Us

Why did you succeed? I worked really hard.

Why didn't you succeed? The weather, the traffic, my computer, the regulations, my boss, my peers, my car, the company policies. I've been so busy! The dog ate my homework. The serpent beguiled me.

This is the Self-Serving Bias in action. A behavioral influence in which we take credit for our successes, while blaming external circumstances for our shortcomings, disappointments, and failures.

Of course we do! We're boosting our confidence while protecting our self-esteem!

There are 2 problems with blaming circumstances:

1. People absolve themselves of personal responsibility. As a result, they become a victim under their circumstances, leaving little room to become a victor over them.
2. People fail to evaluate all the information available to them (internal and external roadblocks), resulting in poor decisions.

As leaders, how do we lead people out of their own way? With the Lasso of Truth. Wonder Woman used a truth-compelling lasso. We can employ truth-compelling questions (just imagine the twirling lasso!):

- What role have you played in your success or disappointment?
- If we look at only controllable factors, which ones attributed to your success or failure?
- From your perspective, what specific actions/behaviors did you take or should you have taken?
- What actions/behaviors can you change moving forward to change your results?

When we allow people to point fingers at external circumstances, we condone their victim status, and they stay stuck. Stuck people, stuck team, stuck leader, stuck results.

But when we help people focus on controllable factors (their actions and behaviors!), we lead them out of their own way.

IN A FLASH!

Fix Those Broken Windows Immediately!

Altercations, missed deadlines, defective processes, and empty promises are like broken windows. Left unfixed, they communicate our tolerance for broken windows.

According to the Broken Windows Theory, addressing petty crimes will prevent more serious crimes. Social scientists contend that small signs of disorder actually encourage more widespread negative behavior.

In 1993, Mayor Giuliani put the Broken Windows Theory into action to decrease crime in NYC. He commissioned the city to remove graffiti, clean litter, repair vandalism, and arrest toll-jumpers. By tackling minor disorders with zero-tolerance, Giuliani reinstated order and lawfulness in the city.

We need to put this theory into action with our teams.

If we don't fix the broken windows, we not only condone them, we encourage greater violations.

By confronting the altercations, enforcing the deadlines, changing the processes, and holding people to their promises, we communicate zero-tolerance for negative behavior and thereby, restore order and justice in the environment.

And, as leaders, the environment is pivotal – it's the only thing we can create. (We cannot control people's skills or attitudes; we can only influence those with the environment we create and the context we provide.)

Consequently, we better be intentional about fixing those windows. Our people are watching.

Chapter 20

HELPING OTHERS GROW

There's Nothing Urgent About Mentoring *(That's Why You Should Do It)*

We just kicked off another leadership mentoring program for one of our clients. And I'm bracing myself for the inevitable. Before the end, someone in the program will confess, "I'm so busy, Ann! I haven't connected with my Mentor."

Of course you're busy! That's how you got into the program. By successfully doing a lot of things – by being really great at your job.

Here's the acute reality: there is nothing urgent about mentoring. Mentoring is important but it is not urgent. And that's why you need to do it.

If you are committed to successfully managing and leading, it's imperative that you learn how to distinguish and serve the urgent (the issues, the immediate needs, the emergencies) while making time for the important.

It's a critical, yet overlooked distinction of strong leadership. So how should we define "important"?

- Growing ourselves and others
- Honing skills and creating new experiences
- Discovering fresh approaches and perspectives
- Collaborating, innovating, and improving
- Recognizing, appreciating, and celebrating others
- Connecting and building trusting relationships

By participating in a mentoring relationship, you have the opportunity to practice the art of intentionally advancing the important while effectively managing the urgent. And if we can learn how to make time for the important-but-not-urgent, you'll have an impact at work (and in life) well beyond your job title.

So how do you advance the important while managing the urgent?

- Find something to care about (what's important to you?)
- Master communications (listening, speaking, setting expectations)
- Learn to delegate effectively (develop, don't dump!)
- Tackle procrastination and time-zappers

Frankly, I don't care if participants accomplish their goals in the mentoring program. I only care that they care. When we are intentional with our time, our relationships, and our communications, we can undertake the important-but-not-urgent, navigate the urgent, and make a difference that ripples.

Stop Giving Feedback. Just be a Mirror.

According to research:

- 65% of employees want more feedback from their boss
- 72% believe their performance would improve if their boss offered more feedback

And yet feedback continues to be hijacked. Why? Because, in spite of its enormous value, it can be confronting. Ultimately feedback reveals us to ourselves. Consequently, people avoid asking for it, while bosses avoid giving it.

Why the antics? Because people assume all feedback is negative (even when it's cleverly labeled "constructive"). And negative feedback feels critical and judgmental.

So what? Get thicker skin, right? Well, here's the psychological skinny on criticism: the brain processes criticism as a threat to our survival. More specifically, when we are criticized, we cognitively feel the threat of being excluded from a group... even when the feedback is completely accurate.

So how can we offer the feedback that people want and need in order to grow, without triggering their fears of being excluded or ostracized?

Be a mirror. A mirror offers a reflection. It allows people to see what they cannot see on their own: their face, their teeth, their hair, their outfit. All without the mirror's judgment or criticism (unless you're Snow White, of course).

As a boss, we can similarly help people see what they cannot see. We can offer a reflection of their actions, efforts, and behaviors that they might not be able to (or want to) see with their own eyes.

How?
- Invite: "Would it help to hear my perspective?"
- Express: "I'm happy about... I'm worried about..."
- Reflect: "I've noticed... I've observed..."
- Involve: "What do you see?"

When we are committed to contributing to someone's success, we can serve as their mirror by offering a valuable perspective, while mitigating the innate fears that criticism triggers.

Managers Grow Like Bamboo Trees

One of my favorite books is *Shoe Dog* by Phil Knight, a memoir about how he launched Nike. It's a must read – I loved it!

In one story, Phil reflects on a moment in Tokyo with Hayami his mentor, in which Phil complains, "We have so much opportunity, but we're having a terrible time getting managers who can seize those opportunities."

Hayami nodded and said, "See those bamboo trees up there? Next year when you come, they will be one foot higher."

Phil understood the message. Bamboo trees, like managers, grow over time, not instantaneously. And impatience will not make them grow faster.

Upon his return to Nike's headquarters in Oregon, Phil prioritized training and long-term planning for his management team, to great success. He realized that he had expected his managers to be successful without helping them grow.

Managers need (and actually crave) development and opportunities to learn. But most development in organizations is focused on new hires, individual contributors, and executives. Whereas, being in the middle often means fending for yourself... in one of the most important jobs in the entire company!

We can do better than that for our managers!

3 ways we can help managers learn, develop, and grow:

1. **Education:** skills and training (i.e., classes, training, books, workshops)

2. **Experiences:** events, occurrences, and situations (i.e., projects, teams, stretch assignments, challenging employees)

3. **Elucidation:** explanations, clarifications, and insights that bolster the education and experiences (i.e., mentoring, coaching, assessments, feedback)

If we need the middle to be successful, we need to prepare the middle to be successful. And if you are in the middle, never forget that it is ultimately your responsibility to seek education, experiences, and elucidation in order to grow your own bamboo.

Stop Kissing Worms

I have a confession... I've been kissing a lot of worms lately. Figuratively, not literally. I keep getting in the weeds on projects – I'm so far in that I'm kissing worms.

For example, Cindy on my team took the initiative to set up a follow-up meeting with a client. I insisted on participating and then I monopolized the conversation. I didn't need to. She is the consummate client engagement specialist.

So why am I suddenly micromanaging? Well if I'm honest, I've been traveling a lot, the team is growing, and I'm feeling disconnected and less relevant. Insecurity is at the root of all worm-kissing:

- We don't know people's skills or experiences.
- We're confounded by the importance of the situation or task.
- We feel left out of the loop and therefore vulnerable.
- Sometimes we're avoiding other aspects of our job where we feel less proficient.

As managers, we're masterful at kissing worms – managing the heck out of projects made us successful in the first place! But the problem with kissing worms:

- Our distrust bruises morale (and breeds more distrust).
- We solve problems for people, which hampers their growth.
- We aren't teaching, coaching, training, or developing.
- We become overwhelmed – with our work and theirs.
- We can't take on new projects or strategize about the big picture.

Granted, some situations warrant our increased involvement, but we can view the weeds without diving into them:

- Agree on a schedule for receiving updates
- Discover people's skills and experiences
- Share context and content
- Ensure people have what they need to be successful
- Encourage questions and ideas
- Allow people to fail and learn

To be a better boss, we must delegate to develop, grow, and recognize people. In other words... kiss people, not worms (figuratively, not literally).

ps. If your boss loves to kiss worms, just commit to over-communicating.

Job Crafting

Coined by researchers at the University of Michigan and Yale, "Job Crafting" describes people who meet the expectations of their job and then find ways to add something that makes a difference and benefits the team/company/customers.

Examples of Job Crafting:

- People who volunteer to mentor others
- Salespeople who solve problems instead of sell products
- People who take on a project for an employee resource group
- My colleague who stayed late to help me prepare for a big presentation
- The Xerox employee who turned an error in adhesives into Post-it Notes
- The Zappos call center rep who sent flowers to a customer whose husband had just died and who was calling to return a pair of shoes he had purchased
- The utility workers from around the country who traveled to the East Coast to help neighborhoods get their power back after Hurricane Sandy in 2013

Where to start? Assess and alter any of the following areas in your job:

- Tasks – what tasks could you perform differently or more effectively? what new tasks could you take on?

- Relationships – what new relationships could you develop and contribute to?

- Perceptions – how does your work affect others? how does your work make a difference?

3 essentials for success in Job Crafting:

1. Create value for others: find ways to benefit and serve your boss, team, colleagues, and customers

2. Establish trust: help others see that your actions are in service of them, not in service of you

3. Start with the yaysayers: focus first on those who support you

Why should leaders advocate for Job Crafting? More than 65% of employees are dissatisfied with their jobs. They're focused on a fixed list of duties. It's time to encourage these people to expand the boundaries of their job description.

Job Crafting: a potent way to empower people to increase their own satisfaction, elevate their own achievements, and improve their own resilience.

The result? Employees who are re-energized and re-committed because they found new ways to contribute and make a difference. And who wouldn't want to work in that kind of culture?

Why this School is Halting Helpful Parents

An all-boys high school in Little Rock, Arkansas has the following sign posted on their front door:

> "If you are dropping off your son's forgotten lunch, books, homework, or equipment, please TURN AROUND and exit the building.
> Your son will learn to problem-solve in your absence."

The school's motto: *to teach reading, writing, arithmetic, and problem-solving.*

In pursuit of that commitment, they are preventing students from being rescued, forcing the students to live with the consequences of a forgotten lunch, books, homework, or sports equipment.

But formerly-rescued students can quickly evolve into victims ("Poor me! No one ever helps me be successful!) or persecutors ("My parents and the school are a bunch of idiots! Don't they know I need my lunch/homework/equipment?"):

Developing problem-solvers involves more than hanging a sign. The school must support students in learning the lesson and accepting responsibility for their own success, instead of shifting the blame.

How do people really learn lessons?
- By doing (or forgetting to do) something
- By recalling and reflecting on the learning
- By sharing the learning with others

As leaders, we need to embolden people to connect the dots between their actions (or failure to act) and the consequences. And we can be most effective when we compel the formerly-rescued to reflect on and share their learning with others. (Hint: look no further than mentoring and coaching!)

Whether we are talking about students or our team, we do our best work as leaders when we stop rescuing people and teach them to rescue themselves

Chapter 21

ROLE MODELS
IN LEADERSHIP

I Have a Leader-Crush on Arkadi Kuhlmann

I admit it. I have a leader crush on Arkadi Kuhlmann, the founder and former CEO of ING Direct.

Why? Because he leads with conviction.

1. He believes passionately that the banking industry needs to be reinvented.

2. So he recruited from outside the industry to infuse the team with fresh ideas and to combat those of grizzled veterans.

3. He then painted a white line outside the building's entrance to remind employees that once they cross it, they are leaving the sleepy world to enter a different kind of place.

4. He also posted a sign above the exit for employees to read as they left work that asked: "Did today really matter?"

5. And to create accountability, every year he asked employees to vote whether he should serve as CEO for another year.

How can we similarly use our own passion to ignite enthusiasm and engagement?

- Start with a conviction (What belief grounds your commitment to lead?)
- Share that conviction until people own it
- Pepper physical reminders of that conviction around them
- Model that conviction in our behaviors and actions
- Ask people to hold us accountable to that conviction

It takes courage to be a manager. It takes heroism to manage with conviction!

I Want to Lead Like Willy Wonka

"I was born to create the unexpected!" declared Willy Wonka.

After seeing the musical Charlie and the Chocolate Factory, I had a renewed fascination with the ethereal chocolatier.

As Roald Dahl's story goes, the greatest candy maker ever awards five children the opportunity to tour his magnificent chocolate factory.

But before they enter, he warns, "You have to believe to see."

Interestingly, on my way to the theater, I noticed a billboard asserting, "You have to see it to believe it."

When did cynicism become our default? We steadfastly disbelieve until provided hard evidence. We watch magic tricks searching for ancient secrets. We habitually question people's motives.

And when we reign with such cynicism, we encourage cynicism in those around us.

As Charlie's story progresses, four children succumb to their greed, gluttony, addictions, and entitlement. But Mr. Wonka finds a kindred spirit in gracious Charlie who believes in the power of imagination to make a difference.

I want to lead like Willy Wonka.

- I want to be less cynical.
- I want to unapologetically create the unexpected.
- I want to believe to see.

By leading like Willy Wonka, I can rouse the remarkable (the "Charlie") in the people around me.

I Want to Lead Like Dallas Cowboys Tony Romo

I want to lead like Tony Romo, the Dallas Cowboys quarterback since 2006.

In August 2017 when Tony suffered a broken back that sidelined him for three months, rookie Dak Prescott was promoted to starting quarterback, but merely as a placeholder until Tony returned.

And suddenly the rookie became a sensation! In that season, Dak led the Cowboys in a phenomenal 10–1 winning streak.

But then people started to wonder... what happens when Tony heals? Will he rightfully reclaim his title as starting quarterback?

Recovered and ready to play, Tony ended the controversy recently in a heartfelt speech:

> "Football is a meritocracy. You aren't handed anything.
> You earn everything, every single day, over and over again.
> Dak has earned the right to be our quarterback."

Imagine watching a younger co-worker soar past us, up the proverbial ladder as we hobble, falter, or idle, unable to contribute as we have in the past. The feelings of futility and inadequacy would thrash even the most confident among us.

It requires an unwavering passion for the purpose of the organization to eclipse the prestige of leading the team to victory.

So what does Tony do now with all of his passion and none of the prestige? Mentor Dak.

> "I was Dak once. I remember the people who helped me when I was young. I'm going to be that person for Dak. Ultimately, it's about the team."

And that's when Tony set a new bar as a leader in the NFL.

If you're truly committed to the success of the team, you lead with heart and soul regardless of who gets the glory.

Do you Exude Courage like Gamecocks Coach Frank Martin?

South Carolina Gamecocks beat the Duke Blue Devils in the NCAA men's basketball tournament in a major upset this week.

But it was the Gamecocks Coach Frank Martin's display of unabashed passion and courage that was most remarkable.

Outside the stadium before the game in Greenville, SC, protestors positioned a large Confederate flag, ensuring everyone entering would see it.

In the post-game press conference, Coach Martin intentionally commented where others might cower.

He could have ignored the controversy. He could have just basked in the glory that his team was headed to the Sweet 16 for the first time ever.

But Coach Martin knew that:
- not saying something would be saying something
- not saying something would be in a way condoning the message
- not saying something would be a missed opportunity

Here are some highlights from his speech:
- "It's [the Confederate flag] unfortunate, but it's America. There are things out there that I don't like. But I can't force people to do what I want them to do."
- "All I know is this unbelievable university and state has taken in a son of Cuban immigrants that's married to a Jamaican woman, has mixed kids, and they've treated me like I'm one of their own from Day 1."
- "I wouldn't want to coach in any other state or with any other group of people, for any other bosses than the ones I've got."

We may not get a press conference for our achievements like Coach Martin, but every day we have the opportunity to exude passion for our work, appreciate our bosses and our peers, stand up for what we believe in, and model courage for the people on our teams.

I'm Going to Follow General MacArthur's Wisdom

General Douglas MacArthur, World War II American General once said, "You are remembered for the rules you break." What rules?

- protocol
- policy
- no-one-does-it-that-way
- this-is-how-we-have-always-done-it
- unwritten team rules
- unspoken family expectations
- society norms

Some rule-breakers we will always remember: Steve Jobs, Madonna, Rosa Parks, Michael Jackson, Martin Luther King, Jr, Albert Einstein. But breaking the rules does not always mean it's legal or even the right thing to do (lest we forget Bernie Madoff!).

Whether it's gutsy or audacious (or even outright rude, unethical, or illegal), those times we break the rules are most memorable – to us and to others.

So how do we pick which rules to break? Start by looking at what's driving our rule-following:

- Are we afraid of getting fired or going to jail?
- Concerned about disappointing people?
- Or just worried what strangers will think of us?

When we are committed to making a difference or contributing to the success of others, we can courageously break some rules. Here are some easy rules to start breaking:

- Conference calls always start at the top of the hour
- Resolutions are only set (and broken) in January
- Resumes never include pictures
- No one writes their boss a thank you card
- Bucket lists are only for retirement
- Don't talk to strangers in restaurants, stores, or the airport

When I look back, the most memorable times in my life have always started with some rule-breaking.

If Only Uber's CEO Had Called Levi's CEO...

Uber's culture was a mess. Complaints of sexual harassment, discrimination, and bullying, multiple resignations, and threatened lawsuits.

Uber's CEO could have used a bit of mentoring from Levi Strauss' CEO, Chris Bergh who shared his approach to culture in The New York Times column "Corner Office."

As soon as Bergh arrived at Levi's, he methodically interviewed 60 people, asking each the following questions:

1. What are 3 things you think we have to change?
2. What are 3 things we have to keep?
3. What do you most want me to do?
4. What are you most afraid I might do?

Bergh gets it. To understand and then influence a culture, we have to connect with and involve the people who are actually creating the culture.

Bergh's ask-the-people approach is bursting with culture-cultivating benefits:

- We gain substantial insights from people in the trenches and on the front lines.
- We communicate the importance of people's perspectives and ideas.
- We help people feel heard and valued for their contributions.
- We demonstrate the power of collaboration to create a culture together.

Typically companies engage in this exercise in exit interviews, but it seems ironic to care what someone has to say as they're walking out the door.

We don't need to wait for an exit interview and we don't need to be the CEO to safeguard and influence the culture of a team, a department, or an organization. We just need to engage with and listen to the people in the culture.

This is our job because these are our people! And so we own the impact of our actions that drive or destroy our culture.

Are we going to Uber it or Levi it?

I Want To Lead Like Yankees Manager Joe Girardi

NY Yankees Manager Joe Girardi made an error.

It was the bottom of the sixth inning in Game 2 of the ALDS against the Cleveland Indians. With two runners on bases and two outs, a batter foul-tipped a pitch off the knob of his bat. The umpire called it a "hit-by-pitch" which automatically walked the batter to first base. Girardi failed to challenge the call as a "strike" (which could have ended the inning). The next batter hit a grand slam, and the Indians eventually won the game.

Girardi was quickly criticized by fans and foe alike. And prior to Game 3 at Yankee Stadium, the crowd (Yankee fans!) booed Yankees Manager Girardi.

His response, however, demonstrated his temperament, wisdom, and fortitude.

He said, "It's no fun to be booed. But [the fans] are passionate and they want to win, and they get upset when we don't win or when someone makes a mistake in their eyes. But you get the good side [of their passion] too. So that's the trade-off. The only thing I can do is give my best to this team moving forward. And that's what I'll do."

Girardi could have met haters with hate.

- He could have deflected attention from his mistake by pointing to others' shortcomings.
- He could have defensively explained how hard his job is and how much he sacrifices to be a manager.

Instead Girardi remained unruffled. He made their boo'ing about his decision, not about him personally. How? By looking for the why beneath their reaction: their passion. He acknowledged fans for it; he didn't make them wrong for it.

It's easy to react with anger and defensiveness. It's even human nature to take things personally.

But it takes a Manager who Leads to respond with maturity, grace, and courage.

Lose (and Lead) with Class Like Penn State Coach Franklin

After a 7–0 winning streak this season, Penn State's football team suffered two back-to-back losses, most recently against Michigan State University. When the game ended in defeat, a few devastated Penn State players retreated toward the locker room without shaking hands with the MSU players.

Incensed, Penn State Coach James Franklin ran after them and made his players return to the field to acknowledge the winners. In his post-game press conference, Franklin proclaimed, "We win with class. We lose with class. And we are going to shake people's hands and give them credit because they deserved it."

Coach Franklin invoked two powerful influences:
1. Social Cognitive Theory
2. Labeling Theory

Social Cognitive Theory: People observe the actions and behaviors of their role models to mold their own actions and behaviors. Children watch their parents. Employees watch their boss. Football players watch their coach.

Through his actions immediately after the game and his behavior during the press conference, Coach Franklin demonstrated for his players the importance of acknowledging the winning team's performance. And he articulated his intolerance for disrespecting others.

Labeling Theory: People who are labeled (especially by role models) tend to mold their actions and behaviors to fit that label. Coach Franklin labeled his team "classy" and "respectful," likely emboldening concordant actions from his players.

We all have the power to influence others with our own actions and behaviors. By:

- exuding passion
- acting with integrity and consistency
- respecting and standing up for others
- recognizing and appreciating efforts
- using empowering labels intentionally

Inadvertently, Coach Franklin demonstrated for the rest of us what it means to lead with class.

IN A FLASH!

Why Cincinnati Reds Joey Votto Apologized to a Fan

Joey Votto, Cincinnati Reds first baseman, was chasing a foul ball heading toward the stands, hoping to catch an out in the seventh inning. Also positioning himself to catch that foul ball was a Cincinnati-Reds-jersey-wearing fan sitting in the first row named Randy.

When Votto missed the ball, he grabbed Randy's jersey and seethed, "You're a Reds fan, don't get in my way!"

Randy the Fan apologized to Votto the Reds First Baseman.

Demonstrating respect and empathy, Randy's apology immediately disarmed Votto's anger. And suddenly Votto apologized too. After the game, the two talked, took pictures, and Votto gave him an autographed baseball that read: "Thanks for being so understanding."

After the game, Votto the First Baseman remorsefully acknowledged to reporters that he had "bullied" Randy the Fan, who deserved to be treated with more respect.

What sparked Votto's epiphany? Randy's apology!

Research shows that apologies have the power to instantly heal. Receiving a sincere apology decreases a person's blood pressure, slows their heart rate, and allows them to think clearly.

Having the courage to take responsibility is extremely powerful. As Randy and Votto discovered, it:

- disarms people
- prevents further misunderstanding
- increases empathy
- strengthens relationships
- fuels self-respect and self-esteem

Authentic and intentional apologies make us strong leaders and decent human beings.

Chapter 22

TEAM-BUILDING

It's Not a Team; It's a Band

Teams win and lose together.

While it's valiant to declare your collection of people a "team," they aren't.

In the end, they win and lose their performance reviews, their paychecks, and their jobs as individuals.

You don't have a team. You have a band.

Every successful band keeps the tempo, achieves harmony, and creates melodious tunes together. And at the same time, each band member can create beautiful music as a solo.

Whether it's a rock band, an orchestra band, a jazz band, or a high school band, band members make music together. And they solo.

What's your number one job as the band leader? Make sure their solo performance enhances the melody of the band.

Let's stop treating these collections of people like an NFL team. And start treating them like a Grammy award-winning band.

It's Not a Meeting; It's a Fitness Class

I've never checked my email in a fitness class.

Why?

Because our instructor involves me and the other participants from the moment it starts. She makes it all about us: our health, our strength, and our safety.

It's never about her, what her boss needs her to do, what she needs us to do for her, or what other stress and pressure she is under. Frankly, we couldn't care less.

Don't hold meetings. Hold fitness classes!

Involve people from the minute it starts and make it all about them.
- Address topics from their perspective and what they care about most.
- Quit talking about you, or what your boss needs from you, or what you need your people to do for you, or the stress and pressure you're under. (They don't really care.)

Whether you powwow with one other person or with your whole team, stop managing a meeting and start leading a workout.

What You Tolerate and Promote is What You Get

In an interview for *The New York Times*, Tae Hea Nahum, managing director of Storm Ventures, questioned the utility of declaring values to create culture in an organization.

Nahum said, "Culture is defined by compensation, promotions, and terminations. Basically, people seeing who succeeds and fails in the company defines culture. The people who succeed become role models for what's valued in the organization and that defines culture."

Essentially, what you tolerate and promote is what you get. Values are aspirational, but people believe actions and consequences over words on a piece of paper.

Social Cognitive Theory says people observe the actions and consequences of role models to mold and shape their own. As an example, if we tolerate bullying, we demonstrate that bullying is acceptable. And when we promote bullies, we concede that bullying is not only acceptable, it's valued.

People will believe what they see, while discounting any written value proclaiming "We treat each other with respect."

When we are too focused on the output – winning a client, making a sale, delivering a report, impressing the boss – we often disregard the outcome. The result: promoting actions and behaviors that are in direct conflict with the ideal culture.

A COO once said to me, "We're not going to deal with the VP's awful leadership style until the body count is high enough." In other words, we're tolerating him until enough people leave. And when his team's turnover hit 100%, she finally fired him.

The COO didn't just miss the opportunity to demonstrate that the VP's behavior is unacceptable; she missed the opportunity to promote a culture of accountability and courage.

Culture isn't written on paper, it's created in our actions and behaviors, including those we tolerate and promote. Whether we run a project, a team, a department, or an organization, stay focused on the outcome, not just the output.

Set the Herd Free

We herd. Cattle, geese, bees, birds, fish, wolves, and people.

We herd, flock, swarm, migrate, school, pack, gather, and crowd.

All of this herding breeds groupthink.

People tend to follow the behaviors, actions, and beliefs of those in their herd to avoid the herd's rejection.

Here's how it works. The herd starts circling around the same idea until it is unanimously embraced. And in the face of that growing consensus, people edit themselves, stifling their fresh perspectives, insights, and ideas for fear of ridicule or rejection.

And then we are left with a group of people who think alike.

Groupthink infects meetings.

Everyone coming to your meeting has unique expertise and knowledge that could benefit the group's decision-making process. But, as research shows, herds are terrible at pooling their information.

Here's why. Meetings are dominated by:
 (1) information that people already know and
 (2) information that confirms the consensus.

As a result, people dilute their contributions and lean nothing new. And we wonder why people hate meetings!

As leaders, we have the power to set the herd free. How? By intentionally blocking groupthink.

Here are 5 practical actions we can take immediately:

1. Ask for Ideas in Advance
Before gathering the herd in a meeting, have people submit three ideas or new pieces of information to help the group make a decision on a particular issue. This will thwart the addiction to pre-existing and consensus-driven information.

2. Brainwrite

With brainwriting, you submit a question or an issue to your group and everyone writes their ideas on paper. Like brainstorming but without the influence of the loudest group members.

3. Assign a Devil's Advocate

Designate one person in each meeting to introduce opposing ideas, views, and perspectives. By assigning this role, you allow that person to contribute alternative viewpoints and positively dissent without the fear of the herd.

4. Talk Last

When leaders go first, people follow. And when people follow, they mute their own ideas for fear of not only the herd but of you. By talking last, you set the herd free to generate solutions independent of your influence.

5. Engage with Smaller Focused Groups

Literally break up the herd. Invite people based only on the expertise, knowledge, and perspectives they can contribute to an issue at hand.
It's easy to manage a herd, but you'll be a lot more effective if you focus on leading the people in the herd.

Stop Making Suggestions

As leaders we have a bad habit. We embezzle ideas. We don't mean to. It just happens.

Here's how:

- Someone on our team offers an idea.
- We look interested and nod.
- And we instantly improve upon it: "Interesting. What if we..."

    (That's what makes us successful, right? We improve things!)

But when we improve someone else's idea, we take away their ownership. Suddenly, it's no longer their idea. It's now our idea.

And our ideas are never incubating ideas. Instead they become directives to our team to execute.

Why does this happen?

We aren't leading. We are managing. We are managing the idea; when we need to lead the person. While we might make the idea better, we miss the opportunity to make the person better.

How do we stop embezzling?

Just smile enthusiastically and say, "Interesting! Tell me more." Let the other person own their idea a bit longer.

We need to stop managing ideas and get back to leading people.

What Are They Not Telling Me?

In law school, we were taught that there are at least five sides to every story: the plaintiff's, the defendant's, and the three people who happened to be walking by.

And the lesson continues to serve: everyone has a different perspective of the same situation.

But people tend to offer us only their perspective when sharing their victim or victor stories. (Not to deceive, but to persevere... it's just human nature.)

What would happen if we considered the other sides of the story instead of jumping to conclusions about people and situations? We would instantly become better leaders!

We just need to pause for curiosity instead of assenting to that one perspective.

We need to ask ourselves:

- What are they not telling me?
- What facts are they omitting?
- What perspectives are they not presenting?
- What spin are they giving me to strengthen their case or enhance the drama?
- What would the other party say about this situation?

When we don't inquire, we risk fueling assumptions, incorrect conclusions, and gossip instead of conversation.

So let's be curious! Let's bring back the conversation. Let's consider those other sides of the story.

It's time to stop jumping and start crawling to conclusions.

The Secret to Surviving Holiday Gatherings and Team Meetings

What do holidays and work have in common?
They are each bursting with people who think and act differently than we do.

The secret to surviving both? Empathy.

The reason empathy is currently missing from our interactions with others is that we judge their words and their actions from our own life experiences.

In other words, we stand on our sidewalk evaluating what they are doing on their sidewalk without ever crossing the street.

People choose their words and their actions based on their own life experiences, their challenges, their fears, their pressures, their beliefs, and their hopes. Not ours.

Empathy:

- does not require us to agree
- does not want us to condone
- does not even ask us to tolerate those words and actions

It only asks us to be cognizant that the other person's divergent words and actions are based on their sidewalk, not ours.

By bringing empathy, we can strive for the patience and kindness required to survive those holiday gatherings and team meetings.

Chapter 23

COLLABORATION

Clarity is the Enemy of Collaboration

In 2018 Amazon, JPMorgan Chase, and Berkshire Hathaway announced a collaboration to transform how healthcare is delivered to their employees. Essentially, they agreed to partner to disrupt the American healthcare system.

Many criticized that they don't have it figured out: big on ideas, small on details.

But that's the secret to fruitful collaboration: go in with ambition, come out with solutions! If we're clear on the details and specifics as we embark on the journey, there's no need or space to collaborate.

The other admonition about this alliance is their utter lack of experience in healthcare to effectively tackle this massive headache.

But that's another secret to valuable collaboration: combine different experiences and perspectives to attack an old problem in a new way.

- Amazon is masterful in removing layers of sales and distribution.
- JPMorgan Chase offers expertise in money and finances.
- Berkshire Hathaway is proficient in investing and business.

Ultimately, collaboration demands audacious thinking from people willing to take a chance and create something magnificent together.

CEOs Bezos, Dimon, and Buffet are cognizant they can solve this conundrum better together than alone. They are already reimagining issues such as lower drug prices, the use of telemedicine, and payment for quality care not quantity of services. And they are inspired by benefiting not only their employees but all Americans with bold new solutions.

At the launch of any collaboration, forget clarity, and instead choose to:

- Imagine new opportunities to disrupt, transform, or solve
- Involve those with deep knowledge, different experiences, and varying perspectives
- Inspire around a collective creed that gives purpose to the partnership

If you lead a team or an organization, you can bolster collaboration by letting go of the need for clarity, specifics, and details. Your job is to imagine, involve, and inspire! From there your people will apply their experiences, generate solutions, and figure out the details.

How Jigsaw Puzzles Improve Our Collaboration

One of my readers emailed me with a suggestion for creating community: jigsaw puzzles! Interesting... why don't I do jigsaw puzzles?

- Arguably, I'm too busy.
- Practically, I want to focus on projects that progress my goals.
- Realistically, what's the point? I already know the end result (the picture on the box!)

As an experiment, however, I bought a 1,000-piece puzzle and dumped it on my unused dining room table... fighting the urge to do something more productive. Here's what I discovered:

1. **Patience.** The puzzle was too complicated to solve at one time. So I played with it in spurts over a month.

2. **Pause.** Turning to it gave me a much-needed pause from the chaos.

3. **Perspective.** I often walked to the other side of the table just to study pieces, progress, and the big picture from a different angle.

4. **Partnership.** Instead of watching TV, my family started helping me, even cheering when we found a missing piece or completed a section.

5. **Practice.** It forced me to practice thinking critically. By definition, critical thinking involves recognizing patterns and understanding how information is connected together.

A Mentor in one of our programs reflected that being a Mentor has taught him to think critically about how he leads so that he can share valuable and practical advice with his Mentee. Like jigsaw puzzles, mentoring and other ways we collaborate require patience, pause, perspective, partnership, and practice.

Ultimately, completing the jigsaw puzzle did not allow me to cross anything off my to-do list. And the final picture was not a surprise. But the experience definitely offered me a new way to strengthen essential collaboration skills.

So now I'll be bringing a jigsaw puzzle whenever I need to encourage people to connect, collaborate, and cheer!

Full Hands in, Full Hands Out (How Restaurants Create Collaboration)

When I ate at Coopers Hawk Winery in a Chicago suburb, I loved it – not just for the food, but for the experience.

Interestingly, the waitress who took our order was not the same person who delivered our food, and a different person cleared our table.

The service was fast; the food was delicious; and we never waited with unmet requests or dirty dishes.

And everyone who came to our table treated us as if we were their customers.

When our waitress returned to take our dessert order, I commented on the restaurant's smooth, almost rhythmic operation.

She revealed the secret: Full Hands In, Full Hands Out

She explained the simple rule: never go into or out of the kitchen with empty hands. Every time you go in, clear a table and bring dirty dishes. Every time you go out, take a dish that's ready to be served and deliver it... even if it's not for your table.

More important than the fast, efficient service, there is an air of collaboration that elevates the restaurant. No one is in competition with anyone else. Rather, they work together to create a great experience for all customers.

And this collaborative culture is not driven by money - they don't share tips. Instead, they share a common commitment: to create a memorable experience for all Coopers Hawk diners.

How can we apply this concept to any workplace?
- Answer a client's request, don't just send her to someone's voicemail
- Share information with other sales team members
- Refill the paper in the copier
- Pick up garbage in the hall, even if it's not yours
- Take initiative to solve a problem affecting all clients
- Make suggestions to improve an internal process that benefits everyone

With Full Hands In, Full Hands Out, we're in this together!

Why Just-Do-Your-Job Won Belichick the Super Bowl

People at my Super Bowl party were starting to leave. The ending was all but inevitable, as the Falcons were up 28–3 in the third quarter of Super Bowl LI.

And then the game got interesting. The Patriots came back with a vengeance, winning 34–28 in the first-ever overtime in Super Bowl history.

We can glean a trite lesson here like, "never give up."

But the real lesson for us as leaders comes from the head coach of the New England Patriots, Bill Belichick whose mantra is: do your job.

Since 2000, he's used this truism to coach the Patriots through 305 games (winning 225) and 7 Super Bowls (winning 5).

There's no greater test for us as leaders than supporting our people from the sidelines... completely unable to rescue them.

What can we possible do from the sidelines? Cheer. Motivate. Yell. Scream. Scold. Cajole. Plead. Berate. Threaten.

Or we can do what Belichick has been successfully doing for 17 years: instill discipline.

"Do. Your. Job." is Belichick's philosophy that reminds his team to:
- worry about your own job, effort, results
- know the guy next to you is doing his job
- count on your peers and they'll count on you

With this simple yet potent formula, Belichick calms his team in the midst of chaos and overwhelm. He uses it to focus them, eliminate distractions, demand readjustment, enlist improvement, and emphasize accountability.

No doubt at half-time, Belichick once again reminded his team to "just do your job."

We lead when we coach our people from the sidelines, and we lead best when we focus them on the one thing that everyone on the team is counting on them to do... their job.to do... their job.

Could Being in Awe Fuel Collaboration?

Do you experience awe every day? The awe from walking among redwood trees, playing with puppies, seeing a shooting star, watching whales off the Seattle coast, hiking the Grand Canyon, dancing among butterflies, and catching a sunrise.

Nice but what does any of that have to do with being a better leader?

Researchers Paul Piff (Assistant Professor of Psychology and Social Behavior at the University of California, Irvine) and Dacher Keltner (Professor of Psychology at the University of California, Berkeley) recently published their research supporting the claim that awe fuels collaboration, promotes connections and bonds, and motivates us to act for the greater good.

So what is awe? Mirriam-Webster defines it as "an overwhelming feeling of reverence and admiration produced by something that is grand or extremely powerful." Researchers Piff and Keltner define it as that "often-positive feeling of being in the presence of something vast that transcends our understanding of the world."

Apparently awe shifts our focus from narcissism to altruism, from selfabsorption to group-absorption. The Researchers argue that awe-deprivation is the cause of a societal shift from "what can I do for my country" to "what is my country doing for me?"

The Researchers argue that we need to actively seek out "everyday awe" such as the nobility and perseverance of others.

If awe fuels collaboration, bonds teams, and motivates people to act for the greater good, then we must intentionally look for everyday awe at work! How?

- Mentoring – when our Mentee takes a chance because of our conversation
- Kindness – when we witness the kindness of others
- Community – when we volunteer and experience the appreciation of others
- Recognition – when we recognize an employee in front of the team and others chime in
- Employee betterment – when someone on the team takes on a challenge and amazes themselves

IN A FLASH!

ABOUT THE AUTHOR

· · · · · · · · · · · · ·

As a former Silicon Valley corporate attorney and a current entrepreneur, CEO, and manager, Ann knows people from many dynamics. Working alongside some of the best and brightest lawyers, entrepreneurs, VCs, and business owners, Ann incorporated companies, negotiated mergers, managed venture-backed financings, and held the hands of many anxious CEOs… and loved it. She then started her own law firm representing over 75 entrepreneurs, grew it until her CEOs became friends, and then sold her firm to a larger firm that continues to represent entrepreneurs and start-ups nationwide.

In 2003 Ann launched MentorLead to bridge the gap between culture and strategy. When mentoring is used as a strategic initiative, organizations can unleash the remarkable in their people… leadership regardless of title. Her programs, books, and speeches tackle ongoing workforce challenges such as: culture and engagement, leadership development, succession planning, integrating millennials, and on-boarding. Her programs are loved by clients such as Kaiser Permanente, Stanford, and Macy's.

As a speaker and author, Ann prepares people to execute powerfully in everchanging environments. From keynotes to leadership programs to executive retreats, Ann turns the kaleidoscope to help audiences see the potential and the power of their role. She is on the faculty of the Institute for Management Studies (IMS) and the author of three books. Her keynotes and books have become popular among companies that are committed to creating and keeping strong leaders and strong cultures in this fiercely competitive marketplace.

In 2012 Ann founded the Mentoring Leaders Circle (www.mentoringleaderscircle. com) where hundreds of program administrators, leaders, and HR professionals go to connect, share resources, benchmark progress, and exchange best practices.

When not on a stage or transforming corporate America, you can find Ann on her bicycle. In the summer 2011, Ann cycled 4,200 miles from San Francisco to New Jersey in The Moxie Ride, to film the documentary, Work Matters, identifying what people love about their jobs and how bosses influence their success. She continued her research from a bike in 2012 cycling 2,600 miles from Key West, Florida, to Bar Harbor, Maine, in 2014 cycling 1,600 miles from Seattle to San Diego, in 2016 cycling 783 miles from Crater Lake to Yosemite, and in 2018 cycling 813 miles from Banff National Park to Yellowstone.

Ann earned the Certified Speaking Professional designation from the National Speakers Association, was honored as a Top 25 Leading Women Entrepreneur by LWE World, was awarded the Outstanding Business Woman of the Year by the American Business Women's Association, and was honored with the Vanguard Award from The McGraw-Hill Companies for her contributions to their employees.

She earned a B.S. in Accountancy from University of Illinois, a J.D. from Chicago-Kent Law School, a CPA from Illinois, and licenses to practice law in Illinois and California.

Other books authored by Ann:

LifeMoxie: Ambition on a Mission! 9 Strategies for Taking Life by the Horns
Moxie for Managers: The Secret to Evolving from Manager to Leader
Why Mentoring Matters: How Smart Leaders Mobilize Relentless Leadership

www.anntardy.com

Ann Tardy

San Francisco to NJ
2011

Crater Lake OR
to Yosemite CA
2014

www.ingramcontent.com/pod-product-compliance
Lightning Source LLC
Chambersburg PA
CBHW081228090426

42738CB00016B/3223